MUCK, SWEAT & GEARS

For Neen, LB and Sid, with love.

First edition published in 2011 by Carlton Books
An imprint of the Carlton Publishing Group
20 Mortimer Street
London W1T 3JW

Second edition published in 2015
Reprinted 2016

A CIP catalogue record for this book is available
from the British Library

ISBN: 978-1-78177-559-2

Printed and bound by CPI Group (UK) Ltd, Croydon, CR0 4YY

MUCK, SWEAT & GEARS

A Celebration of Cycling

SECOND EDITION

Alan Anderson

CARLTON
BOOKS

⊛ WHAT'S IT CALLED? ⊛

The rapid proliferation of bicycles worldwide in the late 19th century posed the same question – "what do we call *that?*" – for the inhabitants of every country in the world. Some of their answers are listed below, along with approximate pronunciation guides and etymologies. Lack of space prevents a comprehensive listing, but these will get you by in several languages spoken around the world.

Language	*Name*	*Derivation*
Arabic	دراجة (darraaja)	
Basque	txirrindu	
(Mandarin) Chinese	自行车 (zì xíng chē)	自行 (zì xíng) "done by oneself" + 车 (chē) "vehicle"
Czech	jízdní kolo	jízdní "travelling" + kolo "wheel"
Dutch	fiets	See opposite
English	bicycle	From the Greek: bi "two" + kyklos "circle"
Estonian	jalgratas	
Finnish	polkupyörä	
French	vélo	From "vélocipède" (Latin for "fast foot")
German	fahrrad	fahren "drive" + rad "wheel"
Greek	ποδήλατο (podílato)	
Hebrew	אופניים (ofnáim)	
Irish Gaelic	rothar	roth "wheel"
Japanese	自転車 (jiténsha)	
Korean	자전거 (jajeongeo)	
Latvian	divritenis	
Lithuanian	dviratis	dvi "two" + ratas "wheel"
Manx	daachiarkyl, daawheeyl	
Polish	rower	From the English "Rover"
Russian	велосипед (velosipéd)	From the French "vélocipède"
Swedish	tvåhjuling	två "two" + hjuling "wheeler"
Thai	จักรยาน (jàk-grà-yaan)	
Vietnamese	xe đạp	
Welsh	beic	From the English "bike"

⊛ MORE RECOGNISABLE NAMES ⊛

The following languages riff on the words for "cycle", "bicycle" or "bicyclette":

Danish: cykel
Italian: bicicletta
Norwegian: sykkel
Portugese: bicicletta
Spanish: bicicleta
Turkish: bisiklet

"The name, like many other words which have crept into our language, is a mongrel, and, as classical scholars would say, should have been written "dicycle" (from the Greek dikuklos (δισ and κυκλοσ), a chariot) or "birote" (from the Latin birotus (bis and rota), two-wheeled). The usage is fixed, however; and we have only to take the word with this definition, and make the best of it."

Charles Pratt (lawyer and cycling advocate) on the word "bicycle" in *The American Bicycler*, 1879

⊛ DUTCH ORIGINALS ⊛

The Dutch, as noted elsewhere, are some of the biggest bike fans on earth. It's surprising, therefore, that noone knows the origin of the Dutch word for bike – *fiets* (pronounced "feets"). Offered etymologies include:

1. A contraction of the French *vitesse* ("speed"): there was a club called *La Vitesse* in Apeldoorn.

2. An onomatopoeic take on the squeak of an un-oiled wheel or chain.

3. A variant on the Limburger dialect word *fletse* or *vietse* meaning to run away or flee.

4. A rendering of the French *vélocipède* (passing through the stages *fielesepée*, *fieselepée* and *fiese*).

⊛ ROVER, *ROWER* AND *PÓBAP* ⊛

A hugely important early bicycle was the "Rover", manufactured in Coventry, England, from 1885. Designed by John Kemp Starley, it featured two similarly-sized wheels and a chain drive to the back wheel and was said by *Cycling Magazine* to have "set the pattern to the world". Starley's Rover is usually described by historians as the first modern bicycle. Such was its success, that in the Polish and Belarussian languages the word for "bicycle" is derived from the name of the machine – *rower* and *póвap*, respectively.

⊛ A BRIEF HISTORY OF CYCLE CRAZES ⊛

1819–21   The *draisienne* (or **hobby-horse** or **dandy-horse**) sweeps Europe and, almost as quickly, vanishes. *Draisiennes* were made of wood and propelled by a seated rider's running feet.

Late 1860s   **Velocipede** mania starts in Paris with the launch of the Michaux pedal-equipped machine. It rapidly sweeps across Europe, Britain and the USA. A welter of books are published in the last years of the decade, the first velodromes are opened, and the first professional riders – male and female – start to appear. Interest subsequently cools as the deficiencies of the front-wheel pedal design become clear.

1890s   The invention of the chain-driven **"safety"** bicycle ushers in the cycling's "Heroic Era". Production went through the roof and intrepid cyclists roamed the known world. The great races were established and the first superstars appeared – men like Major Taylor and Arthur Zimmerman, and women such as Hélène Dutrieu, made huge fortunes and were stars worldwide. The many formats of the road race, cyclo-cross, time-trial and track racing which we know today were codified – along with many which have since fallen into disuse.

World War I and the emergence of the motor car then sent popular cycling into decline. Technical ingenuity was diverted toward auto design: the pace of improvement in bikes slowed, and many

consider that most bikes made in the 1930s were inferior to those produced 20 or 30 years before. Many people still rode, of course, and society was changed by this mobility, but the excitement was gone. Following World War II, the number of miles ridden in Britain fell steadily until the 1970s.

1960–70s   The first stirrings of new ways of riding in America start. In Southern California, youngsters begin performing stunts on modified Schwinn low-riders: this evolves into Bicycle Motor-Cross, or **BMX**, the first new discipline in cycling in more than 60 years. There are models in production around the world by the mid 1970s, and in 1982 the Kuwahara bike featured in Steven Spielberg's *E.T.* turns an entire generation on to the joys of "freestyle" riding.

1980–90s   At the same time, in Northern California, a small group of hippies start to steer old, disposable, "cruiser" bikes at high speed down dirt roads and trails. As the BMX craze peaks in the early 1980s, the first production **mountain bikes** are released and by the end of the decade, the vast majority of new bikes sold are mountain bikes adapted for urban use. Urban bike courier is one of the decade's new career paths and many disciplines of mountain biking are formalized into international competition.

2000s   As road and mountain bikes become increasingly sophisticated (with suspension units, carbon-fibre frames, disc brakes, aerodynamic accessories and so on), a number of everyday cyclists rebel by self-consciously adopting classic bikes and fittings: steel frames, **single-speed** drivetrains (often with fixed rear hubs – **"fixies"**), and stylish woollen jerseys are the order of the day, re-hydrating fitness drinks are eschewed in favour of the ascetic espresso and a clutch of beautiful books are published celebrating the art of traditional frame building. By the end of the decade this has, of course, become quite widespread and – inevitably – much less cool.

◉ UNSUCCESSFUL ATTEMPT ◉

In Britain, the nineteenth century saw a revival of interest in the roots of the English language. One Reverend William Barnes - a keen, if misguided, linguist – was one of many who wanted to cleanse the language of French and other loan words and return it to its Anglo-Saxon roots. To this end he proposed that the bicycle be referred to as the "wheelsaddle". Thankfully, it didn't catch on.

◉ JAPANESE BIKE CULTURE ◉

Most forms of gambling are illegal in Japan: there are, however, four sports which you may bet on: *Keiba* (horse racing), *Kyōtei* (motorboat racing), *Auto Race* (motorcycle racing), and *Keirin* (bicycle racing). Since its inception in 1948, gambling on Keirin has grown to enormous proportions, with over 20 million punters betting more than £9bn ($15bn) in bets every year.

Despite the huge sums of money at stake, there is no pressure on bicycle makers to improve their models and make them lighter, faster or more efficient. The *Nihon Jitensha Shinkōkai* (Japanese Bicycle Association) requires that all *keirin* racers use very similar bicycles, built by a specially-certified frame-maker using NJS-approved materials; wheel size, spoke count, frame geometry, and even weight and material of components are all strictly controlled, so that no rider will have any advantage or disadvantage based on equipment.

◉ *DEKOCHARI* ◉

Sometimes bikes appear that have been creatively customized, such as extreme low-riders, or pimped-up cruisers. The Japanese have raised this practice to an art form with *dekochari*: bikes which have been customized beyond recognition. (*Deko* is derived from "decorated": *chari* is slang for bike.) With shining aluminium sheet mounted on boxy steel frames, sound systems, flags, and huge numbers of lightbulbs, *dekochari* bicycles look somewhat ungainly by day: but at night, when the lights are flashing and the bikes are cruising *en masse*, it's an unforgettable sight – something between a wedding disco and the Invasion of the Daleks. There are numerous *dekochari* clubs in Japan and the first western creations have started to appear in London.

⊛ THE KEIRIN ⊛

The Keirin event was admitted to Olympic competition at Atlanta in 1996 (with the first medals awarded at the Sydney Games in 2000), following a lobbying campaign by the Japan Keirin Association, which donated around $3m (£2m) to the UCI, cycling's world governing body.

This financial support was later investigated by the BBC. Henrik Elmgreen (a Danish former member of the UCI) admitted that, "the Japanese were very influential in the UCI and they offered a lot of money in order to promote this discipline. You can, to a certain extent, say they bought their way in, but on the other hand it is a spectacular discipline."

⊛ DOPING SLANG ⊛

In cycling, most expressions are given in French. Here are three French euphemisms for stimulants taken by cyclists to improve performance:

1. **Le pot Belge.** An unsophisticated and terrifying mixture of amphetamine, caffeine, cocaine, painkillers and morphine that is no longer used by pros, but is reported on the continental amateur circuit.
2. **La topette.** Literally meaning "little bottle", it refers to the stimulants contained therein.
3. **La moutarde.** Meaning "mustard", this is slang for a dose of amphetamines administered at the end of a race.

⊛ DOPING SIDE EFFECTS ⊛

"On seeing me arrive at the hotel, my team-mates started laughing at my briefcase. 'Ah Paul, the briefcase, you're a real warrior alright.' I hadn't got a clue what they were talking about. On visiting the riders' rooms that night, I noticed that many had briefcases. But whereas mine contained my passport and letters and writing materials, theirs contained pills, syringes and little bottles of liquid of every colour and shape."

Paul Kimmage (former pro cyclist) in *Rough Ride*

◉ DOPING LIST OF SHAME ◉

Altering your body's chemistry is one way to improve performance – as legions of professional cyclists can testify. Extremely harmful and to be avoided at all costs, they are summed up on this chart:

Performance-Enhancing Substance	Known Side-Effects
Blood Doping (Used to boost the number of oxygen-carrying red blood cells)	Disqualification
Erythropoietin (EPO) (Used to boost the number of oxygen-carrying red blood cells)	High Blood Pressure, Circulatory Strain, Blood Clotting, Disqualification
Strychnine (Used as a stimulant)	Loose Bowels, Involuntary Convulsions
Anabolic Steroids (In men) (Used to promote muscle growth)	Acne, Aggressiveness, Impotence, Kidney and Liver Dysfunction, Testicular Atrophy and Sperm Reduction, Breast Enlargement, Baldness, Prostate Gland Enlargement and Inflammation, Disqualification
(In women)	Masculinization, Abnormal Menstruation, Excessive Hair Growth, Clitoral Enlargement, Voice Deepening, Kidney and Liver Dysfunction, Disqualification
Amphetamines (Used as a stimulant)	Aggression, Hyperactivity, Erectile Dysfunction, Headaches, Tachycardia, High Blood Pressure, Fever, Sweating, Diarrhoea, Constipation, Blurred Vision/Speech, Dizziness, Shaking, Insomnia, Numbness, Palpitations and Arrhythmia, Disqualification; Death

◉ PRO CYCLISTS AND DOPING ◉

Journalist: Do cyclists take *la bomba* (amphetamines)?

Fausto Coppi: *Yes, and those who claim otherwise, it's not worth talking to them about cycling.*

Journalist: And you, did you take *la bomba?*

Fausto Coppi: *Yes. Whenever it was necessary.*

Journalist: And when was it necessary?

Fausto Coppi: *Almost all the time!*

Fausto Coppi (legendary Italian cyclist), tells it like it was during an interview in 1949

⚫⚫⚫⚫⚫⚫⚫⚫⚫⚫⚫⚫⚫⚫⚫⚫

"My personal take on it is that a lot of the guys who dope actually use it as such a crutch that they stop doing other things."

Dave Brailsford (British Cycling performance director) on doping and neglect of training and equipment

⚫⚫⚫⚫⚫⚫⚫⚫⚫⚫⚫⚫⚫⚫⚫⚫

"I used to take my bottles up to the bedroom and mix my own drinks, then I used to put bike tape round the tops and I put a Rizla paper in the middle, without anyone knowing, so I knew if anyone had tampered with them. I'd give them to my soigneur or the mechanic for the feeds on the road, and I'd say, "If anyone touches my bottles, I'll take you right through the courts." To the best of my knowledge, nobody did. They knew I was a bit forthright and totally against it."

Vin Denson (former pro cyclist), quoted in
Sex, Lies and Handbar Tape

⊛ VELODROMES BEFORE VELODROMES ⊛

The great American velocipede craze of the 1860s (not to be confused with the great American bicycle craze of the 1890s) saw hundreds of riding schools established, where the skills of riding (which included acrobatics, obstacle races, cavalry drills as well as the basics) could be learned from "velocipedagogues". In an attempt to dignify the sport, their proprietors turned to the languages of classical antiquity and venues gloried in such names as "velocipedarium", "velocinasium", "velocipedrome", "gymnacyclidium" and most ridiculous of all, the "amphicyclotheatron". These were thriving social venues – the "gymnacyclidium" (on the corner of New York City's Broadway and 28th St) boasted "over 8,000 square feet for Riding, with Gallery and Seats for about 1,500 people" and was launched in 1869 with an "Exhibition and Hop". It offered indoor riding at the rate of one cent per minute.

⊛ VELODROMES WORLDWIDE ⊛

The website *fixedgearfever.com* is compiling a list of all the velodromes in the world and lists 20 countries with 10 or more in use. Here they are, ranked in order of velodromes per capita of population.

Nation	Number of velodromes	Velodromes per million inhabitants
1 New Zealand	26	6.50
2 Australia	97	4.41
3 France	125	1.92
4 Spain	72	1.53
5 Belgium	16	1.45
6 Argentina	45	1.13
7 Italy	55	0.92
8 Netherlands	15	0.88
9 Germany	52	0.64
10 Japan	127	0.61
11 United Kingdom	31	0.50
12 Venezuela	14	0.48
13 South Africa	17	0.34
14= Canada	10	0.29
South Korea	14	0.29
16 Mexico	20	0.19
17= Russian Federation	12	0.09
USA	27	0.09
19 China	23	0.02
20 India	13	0.01

⚽ FOOTBALL AND VELODROMES ⚽

The home ground of one of France's most successful football clubs, *Olympique de Marseille*, is called la Stade Vélodrome even though it now exclusively stages football and rugby matches. Built in 1937, it originally had a bicycle track between the pitch and the stands – hence the name. This was disposed of during renovations in the 1970s, which is something of a pity for cycling and football fans alike. After particularly momentous victories, supporters of OM would slide down the steeply banked turns on their way to invading the pitch.

⚽ FAST TRACK, FAST-TRACKED ⚽

The first of the new venues built for London's 2012 Olympics to be completed was the velodrome, nicknamed "the Pringle" due to the shape of its roof. Opening its doors in February 2011, it boasted a number of features aimed at making it a particularly fast and atmospheric, track.

The spectators are seated all the way round, creating a "gladiatorial" atmosphere; the air is as warm as possible to help the athletes post record times (air-conditioning in the upper levels of the stands stops temperatures becoming too uncomfortable) and it is naturally lit. It remains the principal indoor velodrome in the south of England after the games, and with a capacity of 6,000, the largest in the country.

The UK's National Cycling Centre, based at the 3,500-capacity Manchester Velodrome, has had a seismic impact on the sport in Britain since it opened in 1994. In the 50 years before it opened, Great Britain's riders had won seven Olympic medals between them; in the following 18 years they won 36 of which 19 were gold.

The world's largest cycling arena is the Gwangmyeong Velodrome at Gwangmyeong in South Korea. It opened in 2006, has a capacity of 30,000, and is shaped to resemble a gigantic cycling helmet.

⊛ LADIES ON BICYCLES ⊛

The arrival of the "safety" bicycle (an early chain-driven bike with two equal-sized wheels) had a huge impact on the independence of women in the Western world. It was a form of exercise which could be undertaken without compromising one's modesty: it opened new vistas of experience; it allowed independent association with other cyclists, male and female. Small wonder that it became a matter of heated debate, particularly with regard to clothing.

The French led the way with the adoption of knickerbocker suits: this outfit allowed Hélène Dutrieu to become the women's world record holder in the hour event, at a time when most British female cyclists were struggling with long dresses, huge hats, whalebone corsets and petticoats. Controversy raged as traditionalists and advocates of "rational" costume (as modern dress became known) argued the case for modesty and practicality respectively. There were court cases when hotels and restaurants refused to admit female cyclists in knickerbockers; one Lady Harburton was driven to found the Rational Dress Society in order to formally defend their rights. However, it was years before this sensible step forward in fashion was universally accepted.

"Let me tell you what I think of bicycling. I think it has done more to emancipate women than anything else in the world. It gives women a feeling of freedom and self-reliance. I stand and rejoice every time I see a woman ride by on a wheel... the picture of free, untrammeled womanhood."

Susan B. Anthony, US civil rights leader

"Under its influence, wholly or in part, have bloomed week-ends, strong nerves, strong legs, strong language, knickers, knowledge of make and shape, knowledge of woods and pastures, equality of sex, good digestion and professional occupation – in four words, the emancipation of woman."

John Galsworthy (Nobel prize-winning author) in *Four in Hand Forsyte*, 1890

❂ MORE LADIES ON BICYCLES ❂

"The bicycle is just as good company as most husbands and, when it gets old and shabby, a woman can dispose of it and get a new one without shocking the entire community."

Ann Strong (journalist) in the *Minneapolis Tribune*, 1895

"She who succeeds in gaining the mastery of the bicycle will gain the mastery of life."

Frances E. Willard (feminist activist) in *A Wheel Within a Wheel: How I Learned to Ride the Bicycle*, 1895

"The bicycle is the most civilized conveyance known to man. Other forms of transport grow daily more nightmarish. Only the bicycle remains pure in heart."

Iris Murdoch (author) in *The Red and the Green*, 1965

❂ LOVING THE BICYCLE TOO MUCH ❂

A Scottish man found trying to have unconventional sex was arrested, tried and sentenced to three years on probation in 2007. At Ayr Sheriff Court, Robert Stewart admitted a sexually aggravated breach of the peace by conducting himself in a disorderly manner and simulating sex with his bike. He was caught in the act by cleaners at the hostel where he lived. Unlocking the door and entering the room, and they found Stewart, 51, wearing only a white T-shirt, "holding the bike and moving his hips back and forth as if to simulate sex."

Sheriff Colin Miller told Stewart: "In almost four decades in the law I thought I had come across every perversion known to mankind, but this is a new one on me. I have never heard of a 'cycle-sexualist'." Stewart had initially denied the offence, claiming it was caused by a misunderstanding while drunk.

⊛ DANIEL BEHRMAN ⊛

The Man Who Loved Bicycles, a 1973 book, has nothing to do with cycle-sexualism. Its author, Daniel Behrman, was a passionate advocate of the bicycle and a critic of what car culture does to human society and health, and his book (now out of print, but readable online) was probably the first sustained argument in favour of steering society away from four wheels.

"I think of cycling as a passion, like love... it's the best sport because it's the most human."

Giorgio Squinzi (professional team sponsor)

⊛ BIKE GEOMETRY ⊛

The geometry of the bike – the angles at which the tubes meet each other, and the tubes' relative lengths – is one of its defining characteristics, as it determines the rider's position in relation to the pedals – and therefore, the way in which the rider needs to move to propel the machine.

The key angle in the geometry is how vertical the seat tube (which connects the saddle to the bottom bracket) is, and a difference of a few degrees makes a big difference. In general, the nearer to vertical, the sportier the ride will be: the rider is pushed forward (producing a more aerodynamic profile) and at the same time is positioned nearly directly above the pedals (allowing them to force their feet downward for maximum power. Time-trialling or triathlon bikes tend to have the steepest seat tube angle. A touring bike, or commuter model, on the other hand, will have a seat post that leans back. This is more comfortable as the saddle is positioned better for the seat bones and it is more stable, as the bike will have a longer wheel base – all helpful on longer rides.

By way of illustration, the seat tube angle of a Colnago C40 (one of the most successful racing machines ever) is around 75.5° (or 14.5° from the vertical). The same angle on the Dawes Galaxy, the classic touring bicycle, is 72° (18° from the vertical). The difference in the numbers seems small, but it translates into a completely different ride.

◉ MAD, BAD AND MADISON ◉

Today's Madison event is one of the most exciting of the modern track disciplines, with pairs of riders engaged in complicated battles that demand timing, teamwork and skill – especially in the high-speed hand-overs that are the event's distinguishing feature.

The early days, though, were very different: the race takes its name from the six-day events that were held at Madison Square Garden, New York City, from the 1890s. The premise of the race was simple, almost absurdly so: competitors had to make as many laps of the tiny, steep-sided track as they could in a single six-day period.

Although the races began in a high-speed blur of collision and injury, they were less a test of athleticism than endurance and will. Deprived of sleep (one hour's rest for every eight hours' racing was considered plenty) and sustained by a diet which would make a modern sports nutritionist weep (coffee, fried chicken, strychnine and cocaine all featured prominently), the riders covered staggering distances under the gaze of thousands of spectators and in a fug of cigar smoke, grilled meat and sweat.

This trial reduced those who stayed the course to physical wrecks: they passed out without warning, lost dangerous amounts of weight and gazed blankly, uncomprehendingly, when spoken to by their trainers and supporters The record distance – 3,360km (2,088 miles) – was achieved by one Charlie Miller.

In 1898, recognizing the inhumanity of the event, the New York authorities ruled that no rider could be in the saddle for more than 12 hours at a time, and the Madison as we know it today evolved: one of the most exciting and unpredictable races that the velodrome has to offer.

◉ MOST-TRAVELLED BIKE ◉

It seems likely that the bicycle that has been ridden the furthest belongs to one Heinz Stücke. After 44 years of continuous touring (starting on 4 November 1962), he has covered well over 600,000km (370,000 miles), wearing out countless tyres in the process. These days he has three bikes: the original machine, and two folding models for reaching less accessible countries.

◉ SIX-DAY WONDERS ◉

The European descendant of the original Madison occasion (as distinct from the Olympic discipline) is the six-day race. Now predominantly a Belgian and German phenomenon, this sees a velodrome in action for six consecutive nights, from about 6pm till well after midnight, with spectators enjoying live music, hot food and strong drink, as well as a series of races between pairs or trios of racers.

Promoters negotiate appearance fees with the riders, which can include unusual conditions: the Australian cyclist Danny Clark would regularly sing while racing to increase his fee. A favourite was "My Way" – an appropriate choice for a man who not only won a silver medal at the 1972 Olympics, but also picked up a clutch of European titles and the Australian Penny-Farthing championship.

British racer Tom Simpson would corner on the vertical advertising hoardings above the banking, a risky trick. The French rider, Roger Hassenforder, would entertain a packed velodrome by riding round it facing backward and sitting on his handlebars: but he wasn't just a novelty act – he won eight stages of the Tour de France in the 1950s.

◉ THE YEAR RECORD ◉

The world record for distance cycled in a year was first contested in 1911; the competition, like many other events, was organized by a magazine – the British periodical *Cycling* – as a means of generating public excitement and boosting circulation. The record has been officially set nine times, as follows:

Year	Record holder	Country	Distance	Distance/day
1911	Marcel Planes	France	34,666 miles (55,790km)	95 miles (153km)
1932	Arthur Humbles	GB	36,007 miles (57,948km)	99 miles (159km)
1933	Ossie Nicholson	Australia	43,966 miles (70,756km)	120 miles (193km)
1936	Walter Greaves	GB	45,383 miles (73,037km)	124 miles (200km)
1937	Bernard Bennett	GB	45,801 miles (73,710km)	125 miles (201km)
1937	René Menzies	France	61,561 miles (99,073km)	169 miles (272km)
1937	Ossie Nicholson	Australia	62,657 miles (100,837km)	172 miles (277km)
1939	Bernard Bennett	GB	65,127 miles (104,812km)	178 miles (286km)
1939	Tommy Godwin	England	75,065 miles (120,805km)	206 miles (332km)

This is one of the more colourful records. Walter Greaves had to ride a specially-adapted bike as he had only one arm; René Menzies rode for several weeks with a broken wrist, and one of his own arms in a sling; and Tommy Godwin's record will never be officially bettered, for the *Guinness Book of World Records* will not endorse any further attempts as this may risk the rider's health.

Godwin's odyssey was notable for the fact that he cycled much of it through wartime blackout (war was declared nine months into his ride) and once he had completed the year, he carried on. In May 1940 he reached 100,000 miles (161,000km): this record still stands. Having spent so long in the saddle, Godwin found it difficult to walk. During the war Menzies (who lived in London) was chauffeur to General de Gaulle.

⊛ MUSIC ⊛

"The bicycle is already a musical instrument on its own. The noise of the bicycle chain, the pedal and gear mechanism, for example, the breathing of the cyclist, we have incorporated all this in the Kraftwerk sound, including injecting the natural sounds into the computers in the studio."

Ralf Hütter (member of the band, Kraftwerk)

⊛ DAISY, DAISY ⊛

The waltz "Daisy Bell" (the chorus to which ends, "But you'll look sweet upon the seat / Of a bicycle built for two") was written in 1892 and was an enormous hit on both sides of the Atlantic. Composer Harry Dacre was moved to write a follow-up, "Fare You Well, Daisy Bell". Others jumped on the bandwagon and there even was a parody entitled "Four-wheeler Made for Six".

None of them had the success of the original, which even became an unlikely hit over 100 years later when it was covered by British band Blur. As a B-side to the single "Sunday Sunday", it reached No. 26 on the UK charts – although it was subsequently disowned by the band's guitarist, Graham Coxon.

◉ KRAFTWERK ◉

Florian Schneider and Ralf Hütter of seminal German electronic act Kraftwerk are both keen cyclists. In the late 1970s and 1980s they would ride up to 200km (124 miles) per day: on tour, they would get off the bus a couple of hours from their destination and complete their journey by bike, and one of their best-selling albums is a collection of soundtracks for the Tour de France. Hütter suffered a serious head injury in a crash in Germany, spending a couple of days in a coma. Happily, he made a full recovery; claims that his first words on coming round were "Where is my bike?" are, apparently, apocryphal.

◉ DEATH TO THE STABILIZER! ◉

No moment occasions greater happiness than a child's first self-propelled ride free of a guiding adult hand but it's often a difficult struggle to get that far and there are usually tears and scraped knees along the way.

This is not the adult's fault, nor the child's, but can be blamed on the tools most commonly used for the job: the so-called "stabilizers" or training wheels. These are an abomination and should be banned: while they enable children to practise one skill (pedalling) they do nothing to help with the main, more important, knack – balance. In forcing the rider to sit passively on an upright machine, stabilizers deter experimentation with the forces of momentum and gravity, which a child has to understand if they are to achieve lift-off. Moreover, stabilizers restrict the range of manoeuvres which the bike can make as they prevent the rider from leaning into the turn – thereby rendering the bike inherently unstable and causing falls.

The solution, happily, is easy, fun and free: take the pedals off. In propelling themselves with their feet, children can get up an impressive speed (which makes balance much easier). They can use their feet to keep themselves upright, at the same time as learning how to lean into a turn, brake and make the tiny, but essential, left–right steers that are the secret of bicycle balance. When all of these skills are learned, re-introduce the pedals. No doubt there will be a few knocks to the shins as children get used to the pedals, but pedalling itself is a simple business and, if the foundations of balance are there, they'll soon pick it up.

⊛ LEARNING TO RIDE ⊛

"It's hard to see how training wheels [stabilizers] can inculcate any of the desired balancing habits."

David Gordon Wilson (scientist) in *Bicycling Science*

"The hardest part of raising a child is teaching them to ride bicycles. A shaky child on a bicycle for the first time needs both support and freedom. The realization that this is what the child will always need can hit hard."

Sloan Wilson (author)

⊛ GETTING HOOKED ⊛

"I was bought a nice racing bike for my 11th birthday and I got the bug... I suddenly thought: 'I'm on my own! My parents aren't here. It's quite good!'"

Sir Paul Smith (cycling fan and fashion designer)

Sue Townsend's immortal creation Adrian Mole perfectly captures the longing for a bicycle so common in the young:

Wednesday January 7th: *Nigel came round on his new bike this morning. It has got a water bottle, a milometer, a speedometer, a yellow saddle, and very thin racing wheels. It's wasted on Nigel. He only goes to the shops and back on it. If I had it, I would go all over the country and have an experience.*

From *The Secret Diary of Adrian Mole Aged 13¾*

⊛ CO-OPERATIVE RIVALS ⊛

"This is the paradox at the heart of cycling: to compete, even rivals must co-operate."

Matt Rendell (journalist) in *A Significant Other*

◉ CORNERING ◉

How to calculate the angle at which you need to lean while cornering? Happily most of us can instinctively perform the necessary sums and on the fly, but if you've not got a bicycle to hand then this equation...:

$$A_L = \tan^{-1}(V^2/gR_T)$$

...should give you the answer, where A_L is the necessary angle, V is your speed, g is local gravity, and R_T is the radius of the circle described by your turn.

Riders who make the move from free-wheeled to fixed-gear bikes should be aware that their ability to lean deep into corners is compromised. On a free-wheel bike, you can either rest your cranks in a horizontal position, or put the outside crank down with a straight leg. Either position will ensure that the crank and pedal on the inside of the turn will be well clear of the ground and in no danger of scraping it, however deep you lean into the curve. On a fixed-wheel bike, though, your pedals will have to rotate right through the turn and if you lean too low, they'll hit the tarmac.

◉ THE UNFORTUNATE DANTE COCCOLLO ◉

One of the intriguing aspects of road racing is the way that the extraordinary demands of the event and the practicalities of drafting, force rivals – often bitter rivals – into mutual co-operation. The riders of the peloton work together for almost the entire distances of the major Tours and classics, diverting their energies to the narrower interests of their team only at critical moments. This necessity forms a unique bond and there have been many instances of collective protest: sit-downs, go-slows and other protests against the media or the sport's organizers.

Riders who show disloyalty to the peloton may also be punished, as the case of the French rider Dante Coccollo demonstrates. One day in 1978, Coccollo dispensed with protocol and broke away from the peloton as it had pulled over *en masse* for a "comfort break". Revenge was not long in coming: later in the stage, Coccollo himself pulled over and riders in the peloton took the opportunity to seize his bike and ride off, dumping it in a ditch a couple of kilometres further on. A humiliated Coccollo was forced to ride to it on the bonnet of the team car and went on to finish that year's Tour only one place in front of the *lanterne rouge*.

⊛ ENEMY ACTION ⊛

"Racers in the peloton are not pals: they're enemies without options."

Paul Hochman (journalist) in *Fortune*, 2006

―――――――――――――

"Professional cycling is a bit of a rat race, but if I'm one of the top rats I can bear it."

Tom Simpson (former pro cyclist)

⊛ THE MONUMENTS ⊛

Storied races with long histories – all have now been staged for over a century – the "Monuments" are the one-day races which the top riders aim to win. All road races, with public courses, they also offer tourists and amateur racers a chance to dream of stardom. In order, they are:

1. **Milan–San Remo** or *La Classica di Primavera* is, at 298km (185 miles), the longest of the professional one-day races still run and takes place every March. The course has seven climbs, but none are especially arduous and the race is often won after a sprint finish between the first few riders to crest the Poggio, the last hill before the line. Two Britons have come first in it (Tom Simpson in 1964 and Mark Cavendish in 2009) and Sean Kelly won it twice, but the dominant figure is Eddy Merckx, who won a staggering seven times.

    In 1910, the race was hit by a storm: the riders had to push their machines through 20cm (8in) of snow and Ernest Paul's feet were so cold that he lost a shoe without realizing. Only four of the 65 starters finished; the winner, Eugène Christophe, spent a month in hospital recovering from frostbite. Despite the threat of such painful conditions, the race was always popular, attracting up to 450 entrants until the UCI limited entrants to a safer 200 in the 1980s.

2. **Tour of Flanders** (in Flemish, the *Ronde van Vlaanderen*). Like the Tour de France, Le Ronde was started by a newspaper editor, Karel van Wijnendaele, and like *la grand boucle* (the nickname for the Tour), it has drawn a population together over the last century. Circling the Dutch-speaking, northern half of Belgium, it starts in Bruges and finishes a gruelling early-April day later in Meerbeke: per capita, it is one of the world's most popular national events as about half of the Flemish population goes out to watch it. It's famous for the short, steep, cobbled hills, narrow and treacherous in Belgium's wet spring weather, that make it one of the most unpredictable of the Spring Classics. Even in these cosmopolitan times, it is usually won by a Belgian.

3. **Paris–Roubaix.** No race embodies the sado-masochism at the heart of cycle racing as elegantly as Paris–Roubaix, which takes place a week after the Tour of Flanders. To some it is known as "The Queen of the Classics" while others call it "The Hell of the North" (the latter coinage dates to 1919, when the route passed through countryside that had been devastated by trench warfare). It's notable for the cobbled (*pavé*) sections of the route, lovingly maintained by a society of volunteers ("Les Amis de Paris-Roubaix"), that jolt the riders agonizingly, sap their strength and bounce their bikes unpredictably. For this reason bikes are

specially set up with stronger, heavier wheels, frames and tyres, and a team-neutral repair car carries plentiful spares for all the riders. The winner receives an unusual trophy: a cobblestone set on a plinth.

"The race is all about surviving, surviving, surviving; I know I didn't feel great, but maybe others felt worse."

Tom Boonen (winner of Paris–Roubaix, 2009)

---

4. **Liège–Bastogne–Liège.** Known as the *La Doyenne* because it's the oldest of the races, this race was first contested in 1892 and takes place in late April each year. (Once again, it was a local newspaper, *L'Expresse*, that started the event as a means of selling more copies: as the paper was a French-language publication, the race is run through the Francophone part of Belgium, and *La Doyenne* and the *Ronde van Vlaanderen* may be seen as complementary events). The outward leg of the race is direct, short and straightforward: the return leg follows a longer route through the Ardennes and with plenty of hills, rewards aggressive riders and breakaway attacks.

As with the other classics, the risk of bad weather is part of the thrill: in 1980 Bernard Hinault beat a field that had been decimated by snow and rain, but got so cold in the process that he couldn't move the fingers of his right hand properly for weeks. Despite this unpredictability, the host nation doesn't dominate this race as they do the *Ronde van Vlaanderen* and it is usually won by a foreign classics specialist or climber.

"Riders who win at Liège are what we call fondisti *– men with a superior level of stamina… it is a race of trial by elimination, where it's very unlikely that a breakaway can go clear and decide the race before the final 100km. You need to be strong and at the same time clever and calculating – in this sense it's a complete test of a cyclist's ability."*

Moreno Argentin (four-time winner of Liège–Bastogne–Liège)

5. **Giro di Lombardia,** or the "Race of the Falling Leaves".
   After Liège, each summer is then dominated by cycling's
   great Tours. The last monument of the year is a return to
   northern Italy, in mid-October. Start and finish points vary,
   but the Giro has many climbs and always visits the hairpins
   up the hill of Madonna di Ghisallo, near Lake Como.

   The great Italian, Fausto Coppi, won the race in four
   consecutive years from 1946–49, and in 1950 broke his
   pelvis in a fall on the race. The finish of the 1983 race was
   particularly thrilling: after hundreds of kilometres of racing,
   four riders (Adri van der Poel, Sean Kelly, Greg LeMond
   and Hennie Kuiper) crossed the finish line separated by no
   more than a foot. The winner was Kelly but the victory was
   not without controversy, for he'd been led out by Stephen
   Roche – who rode for a rival team, but wanted to do his
   Irish compatriot a favour. Kelly went on to win the event
   twice more in following years.

---

*"I think that if I had sprinted in a straight line I could have
won a little more comfortably."*

Sean Kelly (after his 1983 Giro di Lombardia win)

◉ BUFFALO SOLDIERS ON BIKES ◉

As one of the most significant technical innovations of the late-
19th century, the bicycle naturally attracted the interest of the
world's military tacticians and so the US Army commissioned
a special model, the "Spaulding Military", to evaluate its worth
on the field of battle.

Specially toughened to withstand difficult terrain (the
tyres alone weighed 1.3kg (3lb) each), the bikes featured
special mountings within the frames for mess tins and
handlebars adapted to carry blanket rolls. Weighing in at
14.5kg (32lb) each, they weren't speedy, but that wasn't the
point: they had to be robust for they were about to be tested on
very demanding terrain.

A trial expedition was planned for the summer of 1897. A
unit of soldiers – the 25th Infantry Bicycle Corps – would ride

from Fort Missoula in the Northwestern state of Montana to St Louis, Missouri, in the Midwest. Apart from their leader, Lieutenant James A. Moss, all of the soldiers were black, so-called "Buffalo Soldiers", in a segregated regiment; their route would take them through five states and over nearly 3,200km (2,000 miles) of mud, mountain, river and trail. Covering 96km (60 miles) or more each day over hard country, the unit made steady progress; in the judgement of most observers, they covered more ground than a cavalry unit could have.

Such was the interest generated by their exploits – this was at the height of the 1890s craze for all things on two wheels – that 1,000 fellow cyclists rode out from St Louis to meet the soldiers on their last leg and escort them into the city, where another 40,000 spectators crowded to greet them. While their journey certainly wasn't, as Lieutenant Moss asserted, "the greatest march known of in military history", one can perhaps forgive the hyperbole in light of his enthusiasm and can-do spirit.

And the adventure did the *ésprit de corps* of the 25th Infantry no harm at all: one year later, they fought the Spanish at the battle of San Juan, performed with distinction and would report bullet injuries with the heroically laconic line: "I've got a puncture".

American members of late-19th century cycling clubs wore smart military-style uniforms. They also awarded each other military ranks, and used the bugle calls and signals of the US Army's *Cavalry Tactics Manual*.

◉ BICYCLE BATTALIONS ◉

Bicycles were an important means of supply for the North Vietnamese (or Vietcong) forces during the Vietnam War. General Phan Trong Tue was responsible for the 559th Transportation Group, which managed their supply lines down the so-called "Ho Chi Minh trail": this unit included two bicycle battalions. Their bikes were reinforced to carry huge loads (up to 200kg/440lb) and were ridden and pushed along hidden trails through the forest and jungle.

⊛ BICYCLE BLITZKRIEG ⊛

The Japanese Army invaded Malaya in 1941–42 on the back of bicycles. Travelling at speed through the dense jungle terrain, Japanese troops were able to outpace and rout their British and Indian opponents in what has been dubbed the "bicycle blitzkrieg". This rapid campaign (the Japanese advanced 1,100km (700 miles) in 55 days) ended with the shocking defeat of the British defenders of Singapore.

⊛ THE BSA PARATROOPER MODEL ⊛

The British company BSA (Birmingham Small Arms) manufactured bicycles alongside firearms for nearly a century. During World War II, they applied military expertise to a folding bicycle designed to accompany paratroopers into action. The parachute was attached to the wheels and the bike would drift downward upside-down before landing on the saddle and handlebars: they were left loosely fitted in order to absorb the shock of landing.

⊛ HAPPY THOUGHTS ⊛

It is known that the electrical signals around the brain pulse, or oscillate, at different frequencies according to the brain's activity at that moment. The fastest pace, known as Beta (around 20 oscillations per second), is what we associate with conscious thought. Theta (around six per second) is comfortable sleep and Delta (around four per second) is the state of deep sleep. In between Beta and Theta is the Alpha state, between around seven and 14 cycles per second. Alpha waves are associated with light sleep, dreaming and REM, but it is claimed that if you can enter the Alpha state and remain conscious, there are many advantages. Apart from being very relaxing, it seems to make your mind more receptive to new ideas: you learn faster and can think more creatively. Problem solving and concentration are easier and you're more confident to boot.

There are several ways to boost Alpha wave activity in the brain, and alongside the obvious candidates of meditation and yoga are rhythmic forms of exercise like walking, running, rowing – and cycling. The repetitive action of pedalling, linked with the steady breathing this encourages, can, if you're lucky, get you into this highly effective state of mind. Small wonder that thinkers of all kinds, from authors to physicists, claim to take to their bikes when they need help in unlocking a knotty problem.

"After your first day of cycling, one dream is inevitable. A memory of motion lingers in the muscles of your legs, and round and round they seem to go. You ride through Dreamland on wonderful dream bicycles that change and grow..."

H.G. Wells (author)

⦿ LIVE LONG AND PROSPER ⦿

A 2011 report by a British think-tank, the New Economic Foundation, came to the unsurprising finding that cycle commuters are happier than their automotive counterparts, considering "their mode of transport at least as flexible and convenient as those who use cars, with lower stress and greater feelings of freedom, relaxation and excitement". There is plenty of other evidence demonstrating the health benefits of commuting by bike; a huge study in Denmark led by Dr Lars Bo Andersen found that riding an average of three hours a week significantly reduced mortality rates – that is to say, bike commuters live longer. Other studies have found that cyclists make better colleagues, taking fewer sick days than average, having more energy at work and being less error-prone.

"I thought of that while riding my bicycle."

Albert Einstein (on his Theory of Relativity)

Between 2006 and 2010, the number of bicycle journeys taken in Manhattan doubled.

⦿ NEURO MAGIC ⦿

One of the patients of Dr Bastiaan R. Bloem, a Dutch neurologist, made the surprising discovery that despite having such advanced Parkinson's disease that he couldn't take more than a few steps before falling, he could ride a bike without problems. On seeing this, Dr Bloem asked 20 of his other patients – many of whom were unable to walk at all – to try as well, and to his amazement, they all could do this. His results were published in the April 2010 edition of the *New England Journal of Medicine* and occasioned wide debate: it seems that while cycling does not itself cure or alleviate the symptoms of Parkinson's, it does offer renewed mobility and valuable exercise to sufferers. The reasons why, however, remain mysterious.

⦿ THE MAJOR TAYLOR TRAINING METHOD ⦿

Marshall "Major" Taylor (1878–1932) was one of the fastest cyclists of his day, one of the world's biggest sporting stars and while he was racing, the most prominent African-American in the world. With his trainer, Louis "Birdie" Munger, he devised an innovative conditioning regimen that, avoiding "overtraining", enabled him to race hundreds of times a season and defeat riders with much more powerful physiques. You can try it, too:

1. For the first week of training, cycle 5 miles (8km) each morning and afternoon at an average speed of 15mph (24km/h).

2. For the second week of training, up the distances to 10 miles (16km), twice a day, at the same pace.

3. During the third week, start upping the pace each day by 0.5mph (0.8km/h) (so that after three days, for instance, you will be riding at 16.5mph (26.5km/h)). As this becomes more challenging, only raise your speed every other day.

4. After about a month, you will be cycling 20 miles (32km) a day at 22.5mph (36km/h), and your basic training is complete. You may now proceed to working on your fast-twitch muscles, sprint acceleration and explosive power – but that'sa whole other story...

❂ STAY CLEAN ❂

*"I have told Major Taylor that if he refrains from
using liquor and cigarettes, and continues to live a
clean life, it will make him the fastest bicycle
rider in the world."*

Louis "Birdie" Munger (Marshall "Major" Taylor's manager)

❂ THE JACQUES ANQUETIL TRAINING METHOD ❂

If Major Taylor's method seems a little too complicated, why not
enlist the help of a friend with a car and try the much simpler, but
more arduous routine which kept Jacques Anquetil at the top of
his game?

1. Plan a route of about 120km (75 miles), taking in a few hills if
   possible.

2. Send the car off at a steady 55km/h (34mph).

3. Keep pace with it.

4. No slowing down. If bored, why not try leading the car instead?

Anquetil either followed his wife Jeanine, who drove the family
car, or his trainer, André Boucher, who rode a Derny motorbike. It's
unlikely that you'll be able to match the famously bloody-minded
Maître Jacques. Even fellow pros struggled to keep pace after
the first 30km (19 miles) and Anquetil was said to lose up to 3kg
(6.5lb) on each ride.

"A few whiskies, blondes [light] cigarettes, a woman…"

**Jacques Anquetil (five-time winner of the Tour de France)
on his race preparation**

❂ THE EDDY MERCKX TRAINING METHOD ❂

"If the training is hard, the racing is easy."

⊙ THE TOM SIMPSON TRAINING METHOD ⊙

Once established as a pro, Tom Simpson settled in Ghent, Belgium. From here he was within easy reach of hundreds of *kermesses* (local races, raced in 5–10km (3–6-mile) laps) with strong fields of professionals and top amateurs. Simpson would join the race for about 60km (37 miles), forcing a hard pace but dropping out before the final stages. The ride out would be his warm-up, the ride home his warm down.

⊙ THE FAUSTO COPPI TRAINING METHOD ⊙

"Ride your bike, ride your bike, ride your bike."

⊙ THE SEAN KELLY TRAINING METHOD ⊙

*"A rider says to me, 'I go out training two hours every morning.'
But I ask him, 'What about the afternoon?'"*

⊙ BASIC INTERVAL TRAINING ⊙

If you ride a fair distance regularly and would like to increase your levels of fitness, the easiest way is to build interval training into your usual ride once or twice a week. Cycle racing manuals are full of charts and grids or sophisticated intervals which you can build into your programme: here's a simple one to get you started.

Your normal riding style should be energetic but controlled (ride so that you need to breathe through your mouth, not your nose). For six minutes, raise the intensity so you are forced to breathe hard (conversation will become difficult); then, for four minutes, drop into a low gear and spin, without too much effort. Those two phases together are an "interval". Drop two or three more into your regular ride to build up your strength and endurance.

⊙ WINGED WHEELER ⊙

The first human-powered flight across the English Channel was made by a cyclist, Bryan Allen. He pedalled the *Gossamer Albatross*, which clearly owed a significant debt to bicycle design, from England to France in 1979.

⚙ *TRANS-MANCHE* TRIATHLON ⚙

One of the most arduous triathlons is the "Enduroman Arch to Arc" – otherwise known as "London to Paris the Hard Way". Competitors run from Marble Arch in London to Dover, a distance of 140km (87 miles). They then swim to Calais in France, approximately 35km (22 miles) and ride their bikes for 291km (181 miles) to the Arc de Triomphe in Paris. Only six have completed the event: the record, held by Eddie Ette, is three days, eight hours and five minutes.

⚙ THE AMPHIBICYCLE ⚙

No pictures survive of the remarkable tricycle designed by William Terry, which could be dismantled and re-assembled as a boat. The wheels and frame formed the hull: a wooden keel made it stable while air bags on either side gave it buoyancy. In 1883, he travelled from London to Paris using this unique machine for the entire journey: riding as far as Dover, he re-configured it as a boat, rowed over and was promptly arrested by the French authorities on suspicion of smuggling. Having convinced them of his true intention, he continued to Paris by road and canal.

⚙ CYCLO-CROSS ⚙

Cyclo-cross competition (off-road riding and racing) is only a few years younger than road racing: the first French National championships were staged in 1902 and seems to have been popularized, if perhaps not invented, by the Frenchman Daniel Gousseau.

The courses are very compact, normally winding a mile or two around a fairly small area and the riders complete several laps under the very noses of their fans – while the comparative lack of cunning tactics (which is, in any case, the part of road racing that road-side fans rarely get to see) is more than made up for by the sheer energy and pace of the racers and the bike-handling skills on display. The top riders are impressively adept; some are able to bunny-hop a road bike over two 40cm (16in) fences in quick succession on a steep muddy uphill without losing speed.

This muddy, sweaty, action-packed spectator experience is completed by the very vocal support of the fans, leaning over to harangue their heroes at close quarters – often accompanied by the din of cowbells, their traditional accessories.

◉ CYCLO-CROSS ODDITIES ◉

Issue three of *Cyclocross* magazine carried reviews of a selection of... cowbells.

◉ WIND ◉

Wind is fundamentally unfair. If it blows in a 160° arc from behind, it helps, but any other direction – 200° in total – it hinders. So 56 per cent of winds are against you and only 44 per cent help you.

"You never have the wind with you – either it is against you or you're having a good day."

Daniel Behrman (author) in *The Man Who Loved Bicycles*

◉ EARLY MISADVENTURES IN SLIP-STREAMING ◉

As soon as cyclists started to race against each other or the clock, they realized that the greatest hindrance they faced was wind resistance. It soon became common practice in the US for speed record attempts and races to use pacemakers – either "multicycles", tandem-style bikes with teams of five or six well-drilled riders, or mechanical contraptions powered by steam, early internal combustion or basic electric motors. While these allowed riders to reach dramatic speeds in the velodrome, there were downsides and equipment malfunction could cause terrible injury.

The problems were many. Firstly, the machinery was heavy and experimental, and filled with dangerous substances (high-pressure steam, gasoline or battery acid). Secondly, the tyres that they rode on were not strong enough to withstand the high speeds, constant turns and rough surfaces of early velodromes and frequently blew out. Thirdly, there was the risk of other mechanical breakdown. Although these machines did allow amazing speeds to be attained and records to fall, accidents were frequent, nearly always gory and often fatal. One crowd in California was sprayed with battery acid; a rider named Johnny Nelson was thrown off when the tyre on the machine he was following burst and he was run over by another pace-setting tandem behind him; another rider named Archie McEachern died in 1902 when the chain on the pace-setter broke and he ran into the back of it; Floyd McFarland, a champion of the day, was lucky to survive a similar incident.

Looking for a more reliable pace-setter, the American record-breaker Charles Minthorn "Mile-a-Minute" Murphy went so far as to customize a 2-mile (3km) length of the Long Island Rail Road for his 1899 attempt to cover one mile at 60mph (97km/h). He cycled in the slipstream of a steam locomotive on a carpet of boards mounted between the rails; these vibrated wildly, and he felt as if he was riding a wave as the planks buckled and flexed in the wake of the engine. He was also showered by hot embers, but succeeded in his effort. Unfortunately, by the end of the course, he was travelling faster than the train and crashed into the back of it. Surprising onlookers by surviving, he discovered that he had covered a mile in 57.8 seconds. Small wonder the French dubbed pace-making machines *artilleries à pedals*.

⊛ CLIMBING ⊛

"Being a mountain specialist is very hard, not that I'd rather be anything else because I don't think that you can become... well, let's say a better human being, without effort. You can beat the problems of life much more easily if you've met hardship."

José Manuel Fuente (former pro cyclist)

●●●●●●●●●●●●●●●●●●●●●●●

"If the average person could try professional cycling, he'd say, 'My God, I can't believe how tough it is.' Everybody says how tough a marathon is, but 25,000 people show up to start a marathon in New York. Only 200 people can start the Tour de France."

Greg LeMond (former pro cyclist and Tour de France winner)

⊛ NO WINGS ⊛

*"I've read that I flew up the hills and mountains of France.
But you don't fly up a hill. You struggle slowly and painfully
up a hill, and maybe, if you work very hard, you get to the
top ahead of everybody else."*

**Lance Armstrong (former pro cyclist and Tour de
France winner) in *It's Not About The Bike***

⊛ SADDLE SORE ⊛

Being saddle sore is undoubtedly one of cycling's less desirable
side-effects. Modern cycling shorts (with soft padded inserts),
ergonomically designed saddles and specially created ointments
and creams certainly make a huge difference to how severe it
can be, but it still affects professional and amateur alike. Former
French pro cyclist Louison Bobet's was perhaps the worst case on
record (he once required 150 stitches to repair his backside) but
such hardened characters as Eddy Merckx and Sean Kelly were
known to drop out as the pain grew unbearable.

Here are some tips to avoid soreness (in its many forms of
chafing, boils, ulcers and bruising) and alleviate it, if necessary:

1. Ensure your bike is a good fit. One common cause of sores is
   a saddle mounted too high: as you stretch to complete each
   downstroke on the pedals, your hips will rock and move you to
   left and right across the saddle. This rocking causes rubbing,
   which will soon inflame your tender tissues.

2. Shift position and stand, frequently. This will encourage blood
   to circulate all round the region and takes the pressure off.

3. Try a new saddle: one wide enough to support the "sit bones" on
   the bottom of your pelvis, yet narrow enough not to rub your inner
   thigh. You can measure the distance between your sit bones
   (known to medical science as the "ischial tuberosities"): aim for
   these to rest on the padded portions of the saddle. A popular
   alternative is to go for a traditional leather model (Brooks is the
   market leader) which will in time adapt itself to your anatomy.

4. Don't wear underpants inside your cycling shorts; try not to sit on seams of any kind; take your cycling shorts off as soon as you've finished; always wear a clean pair of shorts.

5. Try coating the area lightly with Vaseline or one of the many specialist "chamois cream" products available at your local bike store. These creams are often descendants of potions developed to alleviate sores on cows' udders.

6. Use suspension to smooth out your ride – try a shock-absorbing seat post or a rear shock if you are mountain biking.

7. If symptoms persist, get an expert to assess your bike fit and riding style, then follow their advice. Take any persistent inflammation or irritation to the doctor before a more serious infection takes advantage of your broken skin.

8. Frequent warm baths will allow a boil to drain and by encouraging the flow of blood to the skin, accelerate your recovery.

It is frequently stated that early racers (the Tour de France of the 1930s is often cited) used to put raw beef steak in their shorts, to sit on where today's riders have a chamois pad. Over the course of the day this unlucky cut of meat would – naturally – become tenderized, and the rider would, after arrival, ask the chef at his hotel to fry it up for his supper.

While both the authentic emphasis on a protein-heavy diet and the story's ubiquity suggest there may be a grain of truth in it, it is interesting that no named rider is ever recorded as having eaten cycling-short-steak – or *filet aux cuissards*.

* * *

"There may be a better land where bicycle saddles are made of rainbow, stuffed with cloud; in this world the simplest thing is to get used to something hard."

Jerome K. Jerome (author) in *Three Men on the Bummel*

◉ PARLEZ-VOUS VELO? ◉

The cycling teams that take part in the Grand Tours are made up of nine riders, but not all riders do the same job so must fulfil a number of dedicated roles. As with so much in the sport, the vocabulary for these different jobs is French and for this we should be grateful because the terminology is both evocative and poetic.

The backbone of any team is the *rouleur* (literally, "roller"), whose speciality is covering long distances at a steady pace, at the head of the team, cutting into the wind and allowing his team-mates to slipstream behind. Such is the required combination of aggression and fortitude that *rouleurs* are also known as *bavardeurs* – fighters – and their natural habitat, the *peloton*, is etymologically related to "platoon". On a stage with a bunch finish, the *rouleur's* job is to get the specialist *sprinteur* to the final stretch in peak condition, ready to be escorted out by the *poisson pilote* (the lead-out man, literally, "pilot fish") and launched at high speed in the direction of the podium and its *palmarès* (honours).

In the mountains, specialist *grimpeurs* (climbers) will spring out and use their high-power-to-weight ratio to ascend at a rate that the more brawny *rouleurs* cannot match. The most humble position in the team is that of *domestique* (servant), whose duties involve chasing down inconvenient breakaways, sacrificing their bike when a more senior team-mate requires it and fetching food and water from the team car. This duty gives them their alternative designation, *porteur d'eau,* or water-carrier. In that team car sits the *soigneur* (carer), whose multifaceted role includes feeding, clothing, escorting and massaging the riders.

And which member of the team is the focus of this group effort, this *collectivité*? Sadly, the poetry runs out at this point: he's known rather prosaically as *le leader*.

"French is the only language it [cycling] has ever been written in properly and the terms are all French and that is what makes it hard to write..."

Ernest Hemingway (author) in *A Moveable Feast*

⊕ TALK TO ME ⊕

"As the bicycle banged and jolted over uneven ground,
one yearned for company, for another human whose
conversation would share the anxious misery of those
uncertain hours. Yes, there it was, a vague outline of a
hunched figure swinging and swaying in an effort to find
a smooth track.

French is the Esperanto of the cycling fraternity,
so I ventured some words in that tongue. C'est dur
("It is hard"), but only a grunt came back. For a mile
we plugged in silence, then again in French, I tried:
'This Tour – it is very difficult – all are weary.' Once more
only a snarling noise returned. 'The boorish oaf,' I thought,
'I'll make the blighter answer.'"

'It is very dark, and you are too tired to talk,' I inferred,
sarcastically. The tone touched a verbal gusher as a
totally unexpected voice bawled, 'Shut up, you Froggie
gasbag – I can't understand a flaming word you've
been jabbering,' and then I realized that I had been
unwittingly riding with Bainbridge."

Sir Hubert Opperman (former Australian Champion)
on riding the 1931 Tour de France

As a young pro, Tom Simpson rapidly picked up French: he had
to, as none of the continental riders he associated with spoke
English. He took advantage of this at an English race meeting on
the Isle of Man, telling a group of racers that when thirsty, they
should request not a bottle, but a "b*****ks of wine".

⊕ NEW YORK CITY ⊕

The rolling landscape and winding paths of New York's Central
Park make it a much-loved destination for the city's cyclists. It
has always been so: the park's opening in 1867 was perfectly
timed for the first wave of American "wheelers". Up to 150 of
the city's gentlemen – all men – would train on their ordinary
bicycles and velocipedes at the purpose-built, and magnificently
named, "Velocinasium".

◉ NYC BIKE RACKS ◉

In 2008, David Byrne, one-time lead singer of Talking Heads, designed 11 bicycle racks – unique steel silhouettes, most of which are now installed around New York City. Each is a different shape, referencing the location in which they are positioned. These are the names and addresses:

"The Hipster" (an electric guitar)	Bedford & North 6th St (Brooklyn)
"The Coffee Cup" (a coffee cup)	110th St & Amsterdam Ave
"The Wall St" (a dollar sign)	Wall St, between Pearl & Water Streets
"The Villager" (a dog)	LaGuardia Place, between Bleecker & West 3rd Streets
"The Chelsea" (a standing man)	25th St between 10th & 11th Avenues
"The Jersey" (a saloon car)	9th Ave & 39th St
"The Olde Times Square" (a nude woman)	44th St & 7th Ave
"The MoMA" (an abstract shape)	54th St between 5th & 6th Avenues
"The Ladies' Mile" (a high-heeled shoe)	5th Ave between 57th & 58th Streets

After bureaucratic wrangles, the "New Museum" design was refused planning permission. Another design – of a liquor bottle – was rejected by city authorities for having been "in bad taste". It was to have been placed on the Bowery, former home of the down-market CBGBs bar, where Talking Heads made their name.

"Biking is the new golf."

Janette Sadik-Khan
(New York Transportation Commissioner)

⊛ TOO COOL FOR SCHOOL ⊛

In 2008, *Business Week* (a magazine owned by the then mayor of New York, Michael Bloomberg) selected 20 of the "Coolest Bike Designs". Alongside high-end carbon racers and quirky retro numbers were no fewer than six bikes with electric motors.

⊛ NYC CYCLING OUTLAWS ⊛

In 2010, the NYPD handed out 29,000 tickets to cyclists, which may come as no surprise to anyone who's seen the antics of the city's couriers and food delivery men. In an effort to improve cyclist behaviour and make bad riding socially unacceptable, a high-profile ad campaign urges "Don't Be a Jerk".

⸻

As Commissioner of Police in 1890s New York City, Theodore Roosevelt was quick to see the advantages of the bicycle in law enforcement. His Bicycle Squad were adept at catching up with runaway horse-drawn traffic and on occasion managed to jump into speeding vehicles and overpower reckless drivers. Errant cyclists also needed policing so Roosevelt hired record-breaking cyclist Charles Minthorn Murphy, who was commended for service four times.

⸻

Most cyclists in New York City obey instinct far more than they obey the traffic laws, which is to say that they run red lights, go the wrong way on one-way streets, violate cross-walks, and terrify innocents, because it just seems easier that way. Cycling in the city, and particularly in midtown, is anarchy without malice.

Anon, in *New Yorker* magazine's "Talk of the Town"

⊛ SAFE IN YORK ⊛

Since May 2001, the city of York (not New York) has been served by a team of cycling paramedics. The bikes, most of which are provided free by a local dealer, carry a defibrillator, an airway management kit and various monitors. They have any impressive record, responding to calls in under four minutes – twice as fast as the national standard.

⊛ THEFT ⊛

*"It's one of the worst things in the world to wake up and
not see your bike where you left it."*

Curtis James Jackson, a.k.a. "50 Cent" (rapper)

⊛ BEAT THE THIEF ⊛

Along with motor traffic and its consequent hazards, bicycle theft is
one of the worst problems to beset the urban cyclist. While it will
never be possible to beat the most determined thieves, you can do
a lot to protect yourself and maximize the (admittedly slim) chance
that exists of retrievizzng your machine.

1. Buy a good, brand name D-lock – and consider buying a
    solid chain to accompany it. You'll certainly have to pay
    more than you want: a common rule of thumb is that you
    should spend up to 20 per cent of the cost of your bike on
    security measures.

2. Make a careful note of the bike's frame number, which you will
    need to insure it; and also of the number of your lock, if it has
    one. This will allow you to order replacement keys in the event
    of loss.

3. Consider – if you can bear to – making your bike look ugly
    and less desirable. Some urban cyclists will immediately,
    and crudely, spray a new bike with grey primer, covering the
    manufacturer's decals and hiding its expensive pedigree.
    Others use electrical tape, wrapped around the frame and
    forks, or plaster the frame with stickers. Anecdotal evidence
    also suggests that for some unknown reason thieves dislike
    bikes with drop handlebars.

4. When locking the bike up, make sure that your locks pass
    through the frame and at least one of the wheels – and that
    you don't leave a wheel with a quick-release bolt unsecured. If
    you park up at the same place every day, leave an extra lock
    permanently there for additional security without the weight
    and inconvenience of carrying it about.

5. Pay close attention to the street furniture you choose. A dedicated stand is ideal; the posts of street signs may be nearly as good – but make sure the base is firmly embedded in the ground (otherwise it may simply be lifted out and the bike – and lock – carried away). Also that the sign at the top of it is secure (preventing a thief from simply lifting the bike over the top of the post). Trees should be avoided and railings carefully checked. It goes without saying perhaps that you should choose the most visible and least secluded location you can.

6. If you return to your bike to find that it has developed a flat tyre in your absence, roll it away without hesitation, even if you can't fix the tyre there and then. It is quite possible a thief has let down the tyre to encourage you to leave it overnight, allowing them to work on the lock under the cover of darkness. Take it home if you can and if that's not practicable, moving the bike to a new location a few streets away is better than nothing. The same applies if the saddle has been taken.

"When I was a kid I used to pray every night for a new bicycle. Then I realized that the Lord doesn't work that way, so I stole one and asked him to forgive me."

Emo Philips (comedian)

"Why should anyone steal a watch when he could steal a bicycle?"

Flann O'Brien (playwright) in *The Third Policeman*

⊚ DAMP AMSTERDAMMERS ⊚

Amsterdam is possibly the world's most cycle-friendly capital city – but theft is unfortunately a huge problem, and hundreds of bikes are dredged from the city's canals every year. Barges can be seen with sad skeletal piles of drowned bikes on their way to the scrapyard.

◉ RECOVERY TIPS ◉

If you are unlucky enough to have your bike stolen, there is only a small chance that you will see it again: estimates of the percentage of bikes returned to their owners vary between two per cent and five per cent There are a few relatively easy ways to maximise your chances, though, however slim.

1. Take a piece of masking tape and on it write "this bike was stolen from (your contact details) – call me and I'll be able to describe the bike to prove it". Stick the tape onto the fork steerer tube, where it will be hidden inside the frame's head tube until the bike is serviced. You may be lucky enough to get a call from a conscientious bike mechanic at some later date.

2. Register your bike with any local police scheme: write your name and postcode on the frame in invisible marker (which will show up under UV light). *Immobilise.com* offers an automated free property registration service, which allows police forces to re-unite stolen goods with their owners. It will also simplify insurance claims.

3. Keep a note of the frame number (normally stamped on the bottom bracket): set up internet search alerts to tell you if a bike matching those details is listed on eBay, Gumtree, Bikesoup or Craigslist. At the same time, monitor those sites and search for bikes matching the description of yours. There is a chance that you will spot your machine and be able to recover it.

4. Spend a couple of Saturday mornings haunting the places where suspiciously-cheap bicycles are sold. You may be lucky enough to spot your property and recover it.

5. If the bike is gone for good, try to remain philosophical. This will be hard of course for you have been grievously wronged – but reflect on the fact that bicycle theft is the occupation of the desperate and that most who do it will be feeding drug dependencies. You, on the other hand, are a happy, healthy cyclist, who will soon be back in action on new, and even more beautiful, wheels. Onward!

⊛ OLD GRUDGES ⊛

The area covering Northern France and Belgium is the spiritual home of road racing, but no country has made everyday riding so normal as the Netherlands. The flat terrain and compact towns and cities are perfect for biking about, while nearly everyone rides a traditionally upright "Amsterdammer". During the German occupation of World War II, Dutch resistance fighters travelled everywhere by bike, carrying weapons, secret messages and clandestine materials all over the country. When the occupying German forces realized what was going on, they resorted to mass confiscation of bikes – the largest such theft in history. (Hitler was no fan of the bicycle: he had already banned six-day racing in the 1930s and was a huge admirer of Henry Ford.)

This did not go forgotten. Many years later, the Dutch and West German football teams met in the 1988 European Championships. History, proximity and sporting rivalry combined to make this fixture something of a grudge match and when Holland won 2–1 the nation erupted with joy, people pouring out onto the streets in their millions, waving their bikes in the air and chanting, "Hoorah! We've got our bicycles back!"

⊛ IN FLANDERS FIELDS ⊛

"Flanders is a wild event, deeply embedded in the Belgian sporting psyche and generating crowds similar to a Tour de France mountain stage. The main difference is that everybody is there to watch the race and to cheer their favourites on, unlike the Tour when people often wander out from a nearby campsite, simply to have a picnic and to catch random crap tossed from the publicity caravan."

David Millar

⊛ WHAT'S A FLAHUTE? ⊛

"Flahute" is the Flemish term for riders of particular bloody-mindedness. Windy, with bad roads, nasty short climbs, and frequent rain, Belgium stages its most important races in its unpredictable early springtime, and those who can win those races (and similarly gritty events like Paris-Roubaix) are tough and aggressive – the kind of rider who grinds on over cobbles, through wind and snow, as more sensible riders retire.

◉ BEIJING ◉

Beijing has possibly the worst problem with bike theft of any country in the world and it's widely assumed that it's pointless buying a new bike to ride in the city as it'll just be stolen. In 2006, the city authorities arrested more than 2,000 thieves, but this barely dented the problem; one gang comprised 56 criminals supplying a permanent store. All bikes are vulnerable, even the traditional "Flying Pigeon" model, which is only worth a few dollars on the second-hand market.

◉ PRO HEROES OF WORLD WAR II ◉

The Tour of Flanders was one of the few major cycling events to continue through the German occupation of Belgium in World War II and this caused its organizer Karel van Wijnendaele to be suspected of collaboration with the German invaders. He was banned from working as a journalist until he produced a letter from Field Marshal Lord Montgomery of Alamein, confirming that van Wijnendaele had hidden downed British airmen in his home.

Italian racing legend Gino Bartali, who had won the Giro d'Italia twice and the Tour de France once before the World War II, worked for the Italian resistance. Wearing a jersey with his name emblazoned on it, he was able to cycle anywhere he liked: neither the German occupying forces nor the fascist police dared arrest him for the outcry it would cause – although they knew that the rides he undertook, hundreds of kilometres at a time, were not for training purposes. From his home in Florence he made long journeys as a courier, carrying fake identity cards for Jewish refugees, and on occasion guiding groups of them to the safety of the Alps. In 2010, 10 years after his death, it emerged that he had also concealed a Jewish family of four in his cellar for over a year, saving their lives.

◉ THE ESCOBARS ◉

Cursed by the international trade in cocaine, Colombia has for many years been the most passionate cycling nation outside Europe. Pablo Escobar, the murderous drug lord, was a keen fan (as, incidentally, was Al Capone, who was rumoured to anonymously place huge bets on track races), although his brother Roberto – who also dealt in drugs – had more talent and turned pro. In later years, Pablo sponsored cycling teams, built velodromes and set his brother up with his own "Osito" bicycle factory, all with the aim of courting public opinion and gaining political legitimacy. But this was a doomed enterprise as Colombian cyclists were among the thousands of victims of the Escobars' struggle to build and maintain their empire. Pablo was killed by police in 1993, while Roberto was blinded by a bomb after his arrest in 1992.

⊛ BOGOTAN BICYCLES ⊛

Bogotá is one of the world's most progressive cities when it comes to bicycling. The former mayor of the city, Enrique Peñalosa, devoted cash and energy to building hundreds of kilometres of safe cycle paths and urban planners all over the world should pay attention to his maxim: "A bicycle way that is not safe for an eight-year-old is not a bicycle way". This network is supported by other infrastructure (such as free, secure, cycle storage at railway stations) and the "Ciclovia" weekly event. Every Sunday morning, over 100km (62 miles) of roads are closed to cars and huge numbers of Bogotans take to their bikes to enjoy their roads.

⊛ THE BEETLES ⊛

In Colombia, the local pro racers are known as *escarabajos* – beetles – because of the determination they exhibit in winching themselves up the country's punishing Andean climbs (which crest at far higher altitudes than the *cols* of the Alps and Pyrenees). The winner of the national tour, *la Vuelta a Colombia,* is garlanded in the traditional *collar de arepas* – an edible garland of flatbreads (picture a necklace made of pitta bread, if that translation leaves you baffled). Since the first event in 1951, the race has been won by a Colombian rider every year bar three. In Europe, and especially in the mountains, Colombian riders have also achieved distinction: Luis Herrera's stage win at the Alpe d'Huez in 1984 was followed by the polka-dot jersey (awarded to the best climber) the folowing year.

⊛ BAMBOO BICYCLES ⊛

The American company Calfee produces a bicycle in which the frame is constructed from stems of bamboo, smoked and heat-treated for strength. They are certainly beautiful machines, with a lustrous brown grain, and the company claim that the frames are light, strong and comfortable. They also boast that the carbon footprint of their manufacture is a fraction of that of a conventional metal- or carbon-framed bike, which would make their machines the lowest-emission form of locomotion around. But bamboo is not a new development: it was widely used for spokes in the 1890s and the first bicycle with a bamboo frame was shown in London in 1894.

If you'd rather get to grips with bamboo yourself, you can buy a special kit from Brooklyn's Bamboo Bike Studio, or join one of their workshops and build your frame under their supervision.

⊛ POP A CORK ⊛

The pressure in an unopened bottle of champagne is typically about five or six times atmospheric pressure (expressed as 5–6 atm, or "Bar"). This is about the same as the pressure in a hybrid biker's tyres – somewhat less than a racer would have (typically 7–8 atm), but somewhat more than a mountain biker (3–4 atm).

⊛ TYRE PRESSURE ⊛

There are no hard and fast rules when it comes to the pressure you should keep your tyres at – with the possible exception that a hard tyre is a fast one. Choosing your pressure is a trade-off between speed, comfort and safety. A higher pressure (and today's tyres can take formidable pressures – it's often said that a new tyre will cope with up to double the manufacturer's recommended maximum) will keep a smaller area in contact with the road. This means less rolling resistance, which in turn means you go faster for the effort you put in. This hard tyre will, however, deform less when it strikes an obstacle – meaning the ride will be less cushioned, and you'll feel every bump and rough patch in the road.

Another disadvantage is that the small contact area means that the tyre may slip in the wet: for this reason, racers often let a little air out of their tyres if it's been raining. The cost is a gain in friction (rolling resistance); the benefit is also a gain in friction (grip).

Most pumps sold these days have rudimentary pressure gauges allowing you to ascertain what pressure, measured in atmospheres or Bar, you're running at. As a rough guide for the casual user: 3–4 Bar will keep a mountain bike comfortable and allow its tyres to grip; 5–6 Bar suits an urban commuter or tourist faced with potholes, kerbs and rough roads; 7–8 Bar is the lowest that racers want to be at. In general, if you're heavy, make it a little bit harder; if it's wet, make it a little softer – and, as ever, check frequently and just go with what feels right for you.

If you don't have a pump with a gauge to hand, a firm pinch of the tyre will give you a good idea: don't squeeze the tyre against the rim, but put thumb and forefinger on either side of it.

Check your tyres weekly, along with your chain. Keeping these two components in good order will go most of the way toward keeping your bike running efficiently.

◉ PRESTA vs SCHRADER VALVES ◉

Narrow racing tyres are inflated through a Presta valve: wider off-road tyres, through a Schrader or Presta valve. The lack of an internal spring makes the Presta easier to pump air through than the Schrader; an advantage of the Schrader is that it's compatible with powered air compressors – although it's easy to cause a tyre to explode using one of these, so be careful.

"The type of valve you have on your tyre is determined by the type of fitting you have on your pump. For example, if your pump is equipped with a Presta attachment, then your tyres inevitably have Schrader stems."

Mike Keefe (author) in *The Ten Speed Commandments*

◉ TRANSMISSION PROBLEMS ◉

If you start to notice an "easy" moment on each stroke when you feel no resistance, your crank is either loose or broken. See to it as soon as you can.

If your chain jumps when you put particular effort into a stroke, or you experience sudden unplanned gear changes, the chances are that you need to change it because it has worn out and become "stretched". You can check this in a second or two with a simple tool (a chain wear indicator). A stretched chain will not only be less efficient than a new one, it will also start to wear out the sprockets on your chain rings (the cogs at the pedal end) and on your hub (at the rear). If these sprockets are pointed or hook-shaped, you should change the cogs and the chain: but if they retain their shape, just replace the chain.

◉ THE TRIPLE CROWN ◉

The "Triple Crown" of competitive cycling is composed of the three most prestigious events: the Tour de France, the Giro d'Italia and the annual Road World Cycling championships. To claim the crown, a rider must win all three races in the same year: this remarkable feat has only been accomplished twice to date: by Belgian Eddy Merckx in 1974 and the Irishman Stephen Roche in 1989.

◉ MERCKX WAS THE GREATEST ◉

Eddy Merckx's competitive spirit was legendary: he won the "Super Combativity Prize" on the Tour de France – awarded to the racer with the most aggressive instincts – more times (four) than any other rider. It's not for nothing he was nicknamed was the Cannibal – he was rumoured to have eaten a wine glass for a bet.

The local bike club in Chester, Connecticut, is called the Cannibal Vélo Club. Their jersey is an orange/blue homage to the classic Molteni garb sported by their hero and the club motto is "What would Eddy do?"

"I won! I won! I don't have to go to school anymore!"

Eddy Merckx (former pro cyclist) after his first bike race

⊙ CYCLING AND CREATION ⊙

"In the beginning God created the bicycle, saw that it was good, then went for a nice Sunday ride on the bike lanes He'd made the day before, and they were good, too, because they were new and He had the angels keep them clear of debris. Later, of course, God would get cross and have the flood wash all the good ones away. And God said to Himself, Let us create man, because cycling is too much fun to keep to Myself..."

From *The Cyclist's Apocrypha* (anonymous)

⊙ SAFER WITHOUT A HELMET? ⊙

The good news is that the more people take to the bike, the safer cycling becomes: drivers of motor vehicles treat cyclists with greater respect if they come across them more frequently (and of course, the more people cycle, the fewer drivers there are on the roads).

It is this phenomenon that helps to account for the paradox (observed in Australia) that making bicycle helmets compulsory makes cycling more hazardous. It seems that a large number of people would rather not cycle at all than wear a helmet: because they are not on the roads, there are fewer cyclists. Drivers become less careful, and this in turn increases the risk of collision for those who do venture out. The situation is exacerbated by the scientifically observed tendency of drivers to allow bare-headed riders more room when passing than helmeted riders.

⊛ SAFER WITH A HELMET? ⊛

There is also strong, scientifically gathered evidence that wearing a helmet *does* significantly improve your chances of escaping serious injury in a crash. It's foolish not to wear one, but insisting everyone else must too is not the way forward.

The UCI, having failed to do so in 1991, made helmet riding compulsory after the death of Andrei Kivilev, a successful Kazakh professional, following a fall on the second stage of the 1993 Paris–Nice race. He was knocked out, never regained consciousness and died the following morning.

Tired of the boring design of your helmet? Danish company Yakkay makes a range of cycling hats that may help. This includes the Luzern (a round fake-fur number), the Paris (a peaked cap), the Cambridge (which looks a bit like a jockey's helmet) and the splendidly named Tokyo New Jazz (which defies description). Underneath the covers are discreet, yet fully functional helmets, so the hats combine style with safety.

A large study of bike commuters in Portland, Oregon, found that 20 per cent of the injuries they suffered in accidents were caused by poorly designed or maintained roads: 29 per cent involved motor traffic, and 6 per cent (of which none were serious) involved other cyclists. It was found that the only statistically significant factor in reducing the risk of serious injury was wearing a helmet.

⊛ CAPS AND HATS ⊛

The distinctive peaked caps that pros now wear only on the podium are known to the fashion world by the Italian word, *biretta*. They share their name with the four-cornered cap worn by Roman Catholic clergy.

"Chapeau!"

"Hats off!" (traditional cyclists' congratulation)

◉ PUTTING THE BOOT IN ◉

*"It's a cruel sport, cycling. Chicchi was a fellow sprinter –
by rights we were bound to the same unspoken pact,
the same union. 'Never attack a fellow sprinter...'
B*****s to that. I stepped harder on the pedals."*

Mark Cavendish (pro cyclist)

••••••••••••••••••

*Road racing imitates life, the way it would be
without the corruptive influence of civilization.
When you see an enemy lying on the ground,
what's your first reaction? To help him to his feet.
In road racing, you kick him to death.*

Tim Krabbé (author) in *The Rider*

◉ TRANS-EUROPEAN ROUTES ◉

The *via Claudia Augusta* has a strong claim to being the
world's oldest cycle route: it follows the path of a Roman road,
completed in AD 47 by the Emperor Claudius. Running from
Donauwörth in Germany, south over the Alps, it forks at
Trento, with one route finishing at Ostiglia, the other at Venice.
There are two arduous climbs – the Reschen Pass, 1,504m
(4,935ft) high, and the Fern pass, 1,212m (3,976ft) – but the
modern cyclist may catch buses over them: a luxury not available
to the average Roman legionary.

••••••••••••••••••

If the daily commute becomes a bore, why not try one of the
12 "Eurovelo" routes? These are a continent-crossing series
of cycle paths along quiet roads and dedicated paths with (in
theory) regular opportunities to eat, drink and rest – and no
gradients above 6 per cent At the time of writing the majority
of the following routes are planned, although the coverage can
be patchy, especially in the South and East, so you are advised
to carefully research your route in advance. According to the
Guinness Book of World Records, Eurovelo 12 is the longest
continuously signposted cycle route in the world.

⊛ CHINESE BICYCLE CULTURE ⊛

The sight of thousands of workers cycling to and from work down wide, car-free boulevards was one of the characteristic images of the People's Republic of China. Westerners perceived the Chinese as a nation of cyclists, and so did their leaders. Mao Zedong was responsible for the nation becoming *zixingche de guo* (The Kingdom of Bicycles) in the 1950s and when his successor, Deng Xiaoping, defined prosperity as "a Flying Pigeon in every household", he was referring not to birds but to the most common model of bike.

There are something like half a billion in use in China, many of them variants on the Flying Pigeon. Still in production, this bike is nearly always black, has single-speed gearing and anachronistic rod-operated brakes. Numbers made are declining as the amount of competing models increases: today, 800,000 are manufactured every year, as compared to 3,600,000 in the 1970s and 1980s. But the Flying Pigeon is built to last and the vast majority of frames produced at the factory in Tianjin are still in service.

While China's rapid economic growth has seen car ownership balloon (with disastrous consequences for both air quality and traffic movement in the big cities), the bicycle remains hugely important, both as a form of transport for the locals and as an export industry. The Taiwanese manufacturer Giant, for instance, has nine plants in the People's Republic. The one at Kunshan, in Jiangsu province, will alone produce one million bikes a year by 2013.

"In rural areas, many girls ask boyfriends to guarantee them the 'three things that go round' (a watch, a bicycle, and a sewing machine) before agreeing to marry them. In the cities, from heavy-utility bicycles made in Shenyang to the light Shanghai bicycles, luxury and prestige machines named Swallows, the wide range of models can help you place their owners nearly as exactly as you can European car-owners, Mini or Jaguar."

Pierre Ryckmans (sinologist)

⊛ ANY COLOUR YOU LIKE ⊛

"It isn't a pigeon until it's black."

**Zhao Xue Jie, manager at the Flying Pigeon bike factory,
Tianjin, China, describes the colour options.**

⊛ BAD LUCK ⊛

While today's Tour de France very definitely has its own dangers, spare a thought for earlier generations. Frenchman Apo Lazaridès had worse luck than most: on one solo ascent of the Pyrenean Col d'Izoard, he stopped to wait for company, surrendering a hard-won lead because he was afraid of attack by brown bears. He was unfortunate in his colleagues, too: in 1947, his team leader, René Vietto, ordered Lazaridès to amputate a toe (a procedure that Vietto had already undergone for medical reasons). Like any dutiful *domestique,* he obeyed orders and thereafter walked with a limp.

Following a hunting accident in April 1987 (his brother-in-law mistook him for a wild turkey), Greg LeMond was left with no fewer than 37 shotgun pellets in his body. He was the reigning Tour de France champion at the time but was not able to enter the race for two years. On his return in 1989, he shocked the world by winning it once again.

Many of us have endured the annoyance of minor injury sustained in an accident. Pity NASA specialist Tim Kopra, who in early 2011 hurt his hip in a fall from his bike and consequently missed out on a shuttle trip in which he was scheduled to carry out two space walks.

⊛ ARGUMENTATIVE ADVOCATES ⊛

"Possibly the tragedy of the bicycle is that it was invented too close in time to the car... pedal power hardly got underway before the combustion engine appeared and not only took over the roads but changed our view of machines. We've forgotten that pedal power is a potent form of energy."

Richard Ballantine (author)

◉ COMPELLING ARGUMENTS ◉

Cycling has always attracted the opinionated. In the 1970s – when cycling as a leisure pursuit was in steep decline and racing bedevilled by drug scandal – one of the most articulate writers in the field was Richard Ballantine, author of *Richard's Bicycle Book* and prescient advocate of environmental causes.

The cover shot showed an amiable hippie in an alarmingly patterned knitted jersey tinkering with his brakes, and the book blended hands-on mechanical instruction with rhapsodic descriptions of life on two wheels. "Just as the ideal of classic Greek culture was the most perfect harmony of mind and body," Ballantine wrote, "so a human and a bicycle are the perfect synthesis of body and machine."

The hirsute Ballantine did have a harder side, though: early editions of the book offered surprisingly level-headed advice on how a cyclist attacked by a dog might kill it.

One of Ballantine's spiritual precursors was William Fitzwater Wray, who wrote thousands of pieces about cycling in Britain under the pseudonym "Kuklos". A keen tourist rather than a racer, he wrote weekly for a variety of publications and was also a public speaker on the subject; his passion was for the way that cycling could engage the rider with the landscape and with other people.

His "39 articles of our faith" are a playful polemic outlining the benefits of biking. Here are some of the highlights (you can read them all at *www.cycling-books.com*). If numbers 3 and 4 seem somewhat surprising in the 21st century, remember Kuklos was writing in 1927:

3. Because British bicycles are very cheap, and of wonderful quality.

4. Because British roads are the best in the world, and as good in winter as in summer.

10. Because you can hear the birds and smell the flowers as you ride.

14. Because it is a fine thing to travel by virtue of your own power.

23. Because the cyclist can saunter so slowly if she likes that she can count the bells in the crimson carillon of the foxglove.

37. Because travel is the finest educational system of all; and cycling the cheapest, easiest, and most educational means of travel.

39. Because on every real bicycle there is the unseen pennant of progress, the standard of democracy, the banner of freedom.

☉ RECLAIM THE STREETS ☉

"It is curious that with the advent of the automobile and the airplane, the bicycle is still with us. Perhaps people like the world they can see from a bike, or the air they breathe when they're out on a bike. Or they like the bicycle's simplicity and the precision with which it is made. Or because they like the feeling of being able to hurtle through air one minute, and saunter through a park the next, without leaving behind clouds of choking exhaust, without leaving behind so much as a footstep."

Gurdy Leete (author and academic)

············

"Aren't you sick and tired of having to fight for your life on city streets? Why are we treated like cars by the law, but like obnoxious and unwelcome obstructions by people in cars? Where are we supposed to go? Aren't we doing ourselves and humanity a favour by commuting on bicycle?"

**Flyer for the first "Critical Mass" bike ride,
in San Francisco, 1992**

············

"The best use of a bicycle is commuting, it's not racing or competing or recreation or anything like that. Ultimately its best use is getting cars off the roads."

Grant Petersen (bike designer), 1992

⊛ VELOCIO'S COMMANDMENTS ⊛

The Frenchman Paul de Vivie (1853–1930), who wrote as "Velocio", was publisher of *Le Cycliste*, an early cycling magazine in which he advocated – among other things – derailleurs and bicycle touring. Here are his seven commandments for the wise cyclist, which remain sound advice to this day.

1. Keep your stops short and few.

2. Light meals, and often: eat before you're hungry, and drink before you're thirsty.

3. Never make yourself too hungry to eat, or too tired to sleep.

4. Cover up before you're cold, undress before you're hot, and do not fear the sun, the air or the rain on your skin.

5. Cut wine, meat and tobacco to a minimum while touring.

6. Never force yourself: cycle within your strength, especially early in the day, when a feeling of strength may tempt you to exert yourself too much.

7. Never pedal out of pride.

⊛ WHY DO CYCLISTS SHAVE THEIR LEGS? ⊛

When male cyclists are asked why they shave their legs, they offer a number of reasons why it is worth it. Some claim that it decreases wind resistance; others assert that it makes it easier to dress "road rash" – the ugly (but usually shallow) wounds caused by a spill onto tarmac at speed. It has been pointed out that it's much easier to massage a shaven leg than a hairy one – but the vast majority of smoothly-limbed riders can only dream of having their own *soigneur*.

Most don't offer any other reason than "because I'm a serious cyclist", and it is there that the answer really lies. The hirsute arms of many pros are the giveaway. Every bit as vulnerable as the legs, and aerodynamically significant too, they are allowed to go unshaven. Surely it's because the legs are the cyclist's weapons. A closely shaven pair not only demonstrates commitment to the cause of victory, it shows off muscle definition to best advantage, intimidating the opposition while engendering respect and fear. As Matt Seaton notes in his memoir *The Escape Artist*, "Only someone who is willing to look like a rank novice, a complete outsider or an utter loser, would turn up to race with hairy legs." The resultant psychological benefits are well worth the indignity of picking up the razor every few days through the season.

While there's no risk of leg-shaving vanishing, there are downsides to the habit. Former track cyclist Graeme Obree (never one to pay too much attention to conventional wisdom) points out that body hair helps sweat evaporate more readily, cooling the body more effectively, and also that shaved (or defoliated) skin is more prone to infection when broken. Seaton notes that you can tell a lot about an unknown rider from the condition of their legs: "if they look *cut* or *ripped*, in those expressions which cyclists sometimes borrow from bodybuilding, it is an indication of how low his body fat is. It means he's been training hard. If his muscles are massive and heavy, however, you can bet that this rider has a strong sprint but will struggle when the road goes uphill."

One therefore might argue that the condition of your legs is valuable intelligence for your opponents and best concealed with as much hair as you can muster!

"There was no way I was going to get married with shaved legs in a kilt."

Graeme Obree (former track cyclist) in his autobiography, *Flying Scotsman*

◉ PRO CYCLIST NICKNAMES: FEAR ◉

Jacques Anquetil	Master Jacques (*Mâitre Jacques*)
Mark Cavendish	The Manx Missile
Bernard Hinault	The Badger*
Freddy Maertens	The Ogre
Eddy Merckx	The Cannibal
Henri Pélissier	The Iron Wire
Jan Ullrich	The Kaiser
Roger de Vlaeminck	The Beast of Eeklo

* *"Because it's a devil of an animal to deal with in a tight corner."*

◉ PRO CYCLIST NICKNAMES: LOVE ◉

Gino Bartali	The Pious One
Alfredo Binda	*La Joconde**
Louison Bobet	The Baker of Saint Méen
Laurent Fignon	The Professor
Charly Gaul	The Angel of the Mountains
Raymond Poulidor	Poupou
Ramon Saez	Tarzan
Joop Zoetemelk	The Eternal Second

*Italian for the Mona Lisa

◉ THE LOVE LIFE OF THE CYCLIST PART 1 ◉

"A real professional should concentrate exclusively on his job. When I was winning, I permitted myself one sexual encounter a year."

Alfredo Binda (five-time Giro d'Italia winner)

"My policy is to abstain for a week before a one-day classic and about six weeks before a major Tour. Usually, I am away from home a long time before a major Tour, so there is no problem there."

Sean Kelly (former winner of la Vuelta a España)

(The views of Mrs Linda Kelly, Sean's wife, were not solicited)

"Your wife is your bicycle."

Alphonse Baugé (Marshall of the Tour de France, 1920s)

"Bicycles are almost as good as guitars for meeting girls."

Bob Weir (guitar player for the Grateful Dead)

⊛ THE LOVE LIFE OF THE CYCLIST PART 2 ⊛

*"Here's the routine I'd advise for the evening before a race: a pheasant
with chestnuts, a bottle of champagne and a woman."*

Jacques Anquetil (five-time Tour de France winner)

---

*"When we saw a good-looking girl at the roadside, we'd
say she was 'Campag'."*

**Raphaël Géminiani (Tour de France stage winner, referring to
desirable Campagnolo brand equipment)**

---

*"In 1996 I realised that I didn't have any female friends.
I didn't know a single woman!"*

**Victor Hugo Peña (stage winner of the Giro d'Italia and
la Vuelta a España) in *A Significant Other***

"It's a sport of self-abuse."

Lance Armstrong

---

*"Cycling is much more fun than dating... I still get to chase
women, and sometimes catch them. But when I get dropped,
at least there is no emotional attachment."*

T.A. Melton

⊛ FEMINIST VERSE ⊛

Mother's out upon her bike, enjoying of the fun,
Sister and her beau have gone to take a little run.
The housemaid and the cook are both a-riding on their wheels;
And Daddy's in the kitchen a-cooking of the meals.

Flora Thompson (author) in *Lark Rise to Candleford*

⊛ THE LOVE LIFE OF *MAITRE JACQUES* ⊛

Even in a sport noted for its powerful characters, Jacques Anquetil, five-time Tour de France winner, was unusually headstrong. His racing career was strewn with bloody-minded victories against the odds and he had a difficult relationship with the media, freely admitting to using performance-enhancing drugs and never winning the public's affections in the way that his long-term rival Raymond "Poupou" Poulidor did.

His private life, though, was even more colourful. At a young age he took up with his doctor's wife, Jeanine, who already had two children, Annie and Alain. Jeanine could have no more children and after some 13 years of marriage seems to have steered a broody Jacques toward Annie, then 18, and encouraged her to bear him a child. Thus started a *ménage à trois* which lasted a decade and resulted in a daughter, Sophie, who, while aware of the circumstances, happily regarded both Annie and Sophie as mother figures.

Eventually, Annie tired of the arrangement and moved out. At which point, and apparently in an unusual attempt to win her back, Anquetil seduced her brother Alain's young wife, Dominique. At this point the unconventional family unit fell apart for good. Jeanine also left him, Annie took Sophie in, while Alain moved away and met another woman. After this re-arrangement Dominique and Anquetil had one son, Christopher, and remained together until his death from cancer in 1987. Remarkably, all the members of the extended family he left behind are reported to get on well.

⊛ DERAILLEURS ⊛

Derailleurs (gear changers) made their first appearance in the Tour de France in 1930. The yellow and black bicycles on which they appeared – manufactured by Alcyon to an Italian design – were identically fitted out. Riders were only allowed to personalize them with their own saddle and handlebars.

⊛ ROAD BIKES OF THE CHAMPIONS ⊛

Despite the conspicuous branding on their frames, 20th-century pro riders very rarely used commercially-available bikes in competition. Their frames were custom-made, often in Italy, by expert frame builders, and then painted and branded to resemble the stock bikes of their sponsors. Lance Armstrong has been identified as the first leading rider to use a commercially-available machine (a carbon frame made by Trek in 1999). Bike guru Lennard Zinn also credits the Texan's success with spurring on development in gearing, pedals, bearings, aerodynamics and many other areas – all of which have filtered down to the general retail market. Assuming you have the cash, it's now a simple business to get yourself a road bike in an identical specification to that of your heroes.

––––––––––––––––––––

"The bike is a terrible thing that drives you to make excessive efforts, inhuman efforts. It takes a racing cyclist to understand what it means to hurt yourself on a bike. Apart from that, everything else about cycling is wonderful: the friendships, the tactics, the ambience, the glory."

Jacques Anquetil (former pro cyclist and Tour de France winner) quoted in *Sex, Lies and Handlebar Tape*

⊛ IN HOT WATER ⊛

These days, racers are encouraged to take ice baths in order to recover from a hard day in the saddle and to be in the best possible shape for the following day's exertions. But it was not always the case. Here is one end-of-the-stage remedy, emphatically not recommended, which was in use in the 1950s:

1. Run a bath six inches deep and as hot as you can take it.

2. Add a pint of vinegar (on the Tour, wine vinegar, naturally) and a kilo of sea salt.

3. Soak for five minutes, until the veins on the legs are prominent.

The theory is that toxins left in the muscles after the day's exertions are first drawn from the veins and muscles to the skin, then dissolve into the bathwater. Today's "detox" health regimens recommend baths that work on a similar principle.

⊚ TRICKS OF THE MECHANIC'S TRADE ⊚

While a racer spends the evening after a stage trying to recover with as much food and sleep as possible, his mechanic is hard at work preparing the bike for the next day's exertions. Although all of them will clean, check and tune the ride to perfection, top mechanics have long had a few extra tricks up their sleeve to help their riders have a good day.

1. Polish up a rider's shoes. A perfect appearance will boost his confidence and intimidate his rivals.
2. Make sure that the cranks and front wheel are pristine – the rider will spend many hours with his head down looking at them.
3. If today's racing didn't go well, spend a few minutes changing the handlebar tape. It will make the whole bike seem new once more, and psychologically offer the rider a fresh start.
4. Give the bike a ride to make sure that any refitted components are fitted correctly. Harry Hall, Tom Simpson's mechanic, was once accosted by a suspicious *gendarme* riding around the streets of Marseille in the middle of the night.
5. If money is no object, change the chain for a new one every day.

"We've got this saying, 'performance by the aggregation of marginal gains.' It means finding a one per cent margin for improvement in everything you do. That's what we try to do from the mechanics upwards. If a mechanic sticks a tyre on, and someone comes along and says it could be done better, it's not an insult – it's because we are always striving for improvement, for those one per cent gains, in absolutely every single thing we do."

Dave Brailsford (British Cycling performance director)

⊚ AFFORDABLE UPGRADES AND FIXES ⊚

1. **Replace the jockey wheels.** The small wheels that guide the chain through the cage of your rear derailleur are known as "jockey wheels". If your transmission is noisy or feels rough at that point, try replacing these before you replace the whole derailleur. They are a fraction of the cost – although as always with cycling components, it's easy enough to spend a

fortune on them if you're so inclined – and as they take more punishment than any other part of the drivetrain, it may well solve your problem.

2. **Adjust your handlebars.** Have a good look at the handlebars that came with your bike – are they comfortable? There are a huge wealth of shapes and sizes available and by adopting a new position, you may find that you're suddenly much more comfortable. The American designer Grant Petersen is a passionate advocate of experimentation with different shapes and most simply, raising the bars to a more comfortable level – as he puts it, "Handlebars too low cause 90 per cent of the discomfort people suffer."

3. **Buy a chain bath.** By letting you thoroughly, rapidly, clean your chain without taking it off, a chain bath will save you many hours of ineffective fiddling with an old toothbrush and make a huge difference to your efficiency.

4. **Change the stem.** An easy component to change if you think your bike could be more comfortable is the handlebar stem. If you feel stretched forward, try a stem that brings your handlebars nearer to you. But if you feel squashed up, try the reverse. You may have an adjustable stem allowing a wide range of positions, in which case this is a free fix – but even a whole new stem is a comparatively cheap component.

5. **Adjust the saddle.** A small adjustment that can make a big difference to comfort is saddle position. Try shifting it forward or back on its guide rails, or up and down on its post – even a movement of a few millimetres will make a perceptible difference, and it's free. You'll be in good company – many pro riders fiddle with their saddles – even during a race.

⊛ BIKE CHECK-UPS ⊛

Whenever you buy a new bike, or have an old one serviced, pay particular care for the first few miles you're riding it. This is the period when problems most often arise; newly fitted parts may work loose, or fail altogether. In particular, every time you get your bike back from a service, double-check the brakes. A good bike shop will give you a free check-up a few weeks after you buy a new machine. If they don't offer you this service when you're purchasing it, ask for one – and if they refuse, consider taking your business elsewhere.

☀ SOME ABBREVIATIONS ☀

The world of the bike is beset with abbreviations. Here are some of the most common:

ASO   Amaury Sport Organisation. The company which organizes and promotes the Tour de France (alongside many other bike races, equestrian events and the French Tennis Open)

BLRC   The British League of Racing Cyclists

BSO   "Bicycle Shaped Object". This is a euphemism for what you may get if you are unwise enough to seek a bargain at a non-specialist chain retailer. It will look fine at first, but don't trust it until you've given it a thorough pre-ride service to make sure that it's been properly put together and the componentry is up to the job. Horror stories of badly-fitted, fragile or missing parts abound.

CTC   The Cyclist's Touring Club. The UK's largest bike organization, it has recently achieved a record high in membership.

CTT   Cycling Time Trials

LBS   "Local Bike Shop". Usually considered the best place to buy a bike and to avoid buying a BSO (see above).

NCU   The National Cycling Union. Once banned former pro cyclist Tom Simpson for six months for failing to obey a stop sign.

SPD   "Shimano Pedalling Dynamics". These arrived some years after the first clipless pedal-plus-cleat model (manufactured by Cinelli). The SPD is now the industry standard for mountain bike and commuter pedals, and a road racing version is popular, too.

UCI   The Union Cycliste Internationale, the sport's world governing body. Responsible for determining, among other things, which bikes and riding positions are legal in which events – and, on occasion, changing these rules in the middle of the night without telling anyone.

VCL   Vélo Club Londres. Just as some continental football clubs adopted the English initials "FC" to denote an affinity with the English origins of that sport, so many English cycling clubs are styled VC or Vélo Club, in recognition of the Francophone origins of serious cycle sport.

◉ CYCLING FASHIONISTAS ◉

The fashion world – particularly the Italian fashion world – has occasionally dabbled in cycling. The expression *bella in sella* refers to being well turned out in the saddle and stylish Milanese jerseys and kit are sought-after worldwide.

Giorgio Armani launched the Armani Sportbike in 2005 – according to its riders, an unexceptional aluminium hybrid, with no unusual features except an iPod holder and a magnetic appeal to bike thieves. Armani claimed the very first one on display was stolen from Caesar's Palace, Las Vegas by a team of criminals in a mysterious black helicopter. This story, which gained the bike widespread media coverage, is regarded with some scepticism.

The English label Rapha – specializing in high-end, stylish cycle wear – was launched in 2004 with the support of menswear legend Sir Paul Smith and, since 2006, has run the Smithfield Nocturne, London's own criterium race.

In 2008 French label Hermès teamed up with Heerenveen-based manufacturer Batavus to launch a £2,200 ($3,500) "Old Dutch" model. Remarkably similar to Batavus bikes available at a quarter of the price, the "Old Dutch" featured tubes that were finished in hand-stitched leather.

Finally, if proof were needed of the bicycle's recent hipness, it came with the 2009 announcement that Urban Outfitters – a fashion chain – would stock single-speed "track" bikes. As one would perhaps expect, a significant number of reviewers filed the machines under the "BSO" category (see opposite for a list of acronyms).

━━━━━━━━━━━━━━━━━

I was style-conscious, because how the bike looked and how you looked on the bike were very important. They probably weren't, but it felt like they were. I remember when I started racing there was one boy who nearly always won and he'd got black socks instead of white socks. Me and my f riends were harassed by that: 'How could he win? He's got black socks!'

Sir Paul Smith (cycling fan and fashion designer)

⊛ LYCRA, MATERIAL OF WONDER ⊛

Lycra was invented in 1958 by Joseph Shivers at DuPont's laboratories in Virginia, USA and has one fantastically useful property: elasticity. A piece can be stretched up to seven times its length without breaking or distorting. Cycling clothing was transformed by the introduction of a small amount of Lycra to the weave: not only does it keep a smooth, aerodynamic profile, it compresses the muscles slightly, reducing fatigue. It is also known as spandex – an anagram of "expands".

⊛ WOOL, MATERIAL OF WONDER, TOO ⊛

Until comparatively recently, most cycling jerseys were made of wool. Naturally breathable, it is also elastic and good for a wide range of temperatures, although itchiness may be a problem. One huge advantage it has over synthetic fabrics is that it does not start to smell for a long time. These days, pros wear sophisticated polyester shirts. These are light, aerodynamic and (unlike wool) do not turn heavy when wet. Microfibre weaves wick moisture away from the skin, letting the rider cool down efficiently – although you will still want to wash them immediately after a warm ride.

⊛ ALL THE GEAR ⊛

"With the heaps of overly specialized gear – gloves, shoes, and biking jerseys – most cyclists realize that every day on the road is Halloween. Plain and simple, it's wearing a costume each time out of the gate....We're neon signs, stylistically impaired wonders blinding pedestrians and fooling small children into thinking that the circus has come back to town."

Joe Kurmaskie (author) in The Metal Cowboy:
Riding Outside the Lines

⊛ THE TWEED RUN ⊛

If you're a stylish dresser, London's annual Tweed Run, which bills itself as "A Metropolitan Bicycle Ride with a Bit of Style" may be just the ticket. Vintage bicycles are welcomed on the 16km

(10-mile) circuit and vintage clothing is compulsory. Riders sport: "Tweed suits, plus fours, bowties, cycling capes and jaunty flat caps". There are no prizes for rapid completion of the course, although there is a competition – open to men and women – for the wearer of the best moustache.

✪ UGH ✪

"As for the racing jerseys and shorts, these were quite the stuff of horror stories. All wool construction, the jerseys bagged and sagged in a disgusting manner, and when wet were horrid. Shorts, also wool – a compulsory black – were even worse when wet, with a real chamois lining which became a slimy mess, heavy and saggy they ruined many a young man's dream."

Pam Manser, English cyclist and roads campaigner

✪ FIGHT THE GOOD FIGHT ✪

One of the honours in the Tour de France depends not on an objectively-measured result, points total or race time, but the opinion of a committee of eight experts. This is the "Combativity Award", given each day to the racer who, in the opinion of the judges, has done most to force the pace, break the race up, make it unpredictable and (a cynic might say) give the TV cameras something to look at while the serious contenders for the General Classification lurk in the peloton, keeping a careful eye on each other for mile after mile.

The daily prize, worth €2,000 (£1,800/$2,900), is awarded after every stage apart from time-trials. The "Super Combativity Award", worth ten times this amount, is awarded at the end of the Tour. The winner of the previous day's prize wears a *dossard* (race number) featuring white numbers on a red background (not the usual black number on a white background).

✪ YOU HEARD IT ON THE RADIO ✪

Radio Tour is the short-wave radio station that broadcasts from the front of the race and is listened to in the team cars behind. The riders are always referred to by the number of their *dossard*, not their names.

⊛ STAYING IN TOUCH ⊛

London-based community radio station Resonance FM is one of the very few broadcasters in the world to devote regular airtime to cycling matters. *The Bike Show*, presented by Jack Thurston, has a wide-ranging approach, covering issues as diverse as frame building, the major Tours, bike lanes and any kind of event with a connection to life on two wheels. Although Resonance FM is only available in the capital, the programme is nearly always of interest to riders everywhere and it may be downloaded as a podcast – so there's no reason not to listen in. And the music selections are great, too.

⊛ FRAME MATERIALS ⊛

A bicycle frame may be judged by three criteria: weight, flexibility (or its opposite, stiffness) and strength. These are your options:

1. **Steel.** For the better part of a century, nearly all bike frames were made from steel tubing: comparatively heavy, but flexible and strong enough for thin tube walls to work well. This continues to make steel (often alloyed with chromium, vanadium or molybdenum) the ideal material where comfort and durability are an issue.

   The frame will soak up some vibration from the road, giving you a comfortable ride, and there's plenty of flex if you hit a pothole or a kerb. However, this flexibility also drains a little of the power of your stroke and of course the weight slows you down, too.

   Finally, steel is resistant to "fatigue" (fatigue causes frames to crack due to repeated stresses placed on the tubing). So, as long as it doesn't rust, a steel frame should last you a lifetime.

2. **Aluminium.** The first of these were manufactured in the 1890s but they did not become practical until the 1970s since aluminium is much more difficult to work with than steel. While it's a much lighter metal, it's weaker and especially susceptible to fatigue – so in order to make a bicycle frame that's as strong as a steel one, it's necessary to use nearly the same weight of metal. This will, however, result in a much stiffer bike. The

contrast in properties means that aluminium has been used in many racing bikes, which need to be light and stiff but not comfortable or durable in the very long term. Plus, it's cheap.

3. **Magnesium.** Lighter even than aluminium is magnesium, which is also strong: it does have the significant disadvantage of being very reactive with oxygen. This means that the frames have to be carefully coated, especially where other metal componentry meets the frame. So, while a magnesium bike may help you win races, it's unlikely to last you a lifetime.

4. **Titanium.** Probably the most desirable of all metals for frame-building. This combines the best qualities of both aluminium and steel. Like the former, it's light, completely resistant to corrosion and cheap; like the latter, it can be flexible and strong.

    The downside is that it's very difficult to work with as it has to be welded in a super-clean atmosphere of inert gas – meaning that the welder needs to work while looking at the frame through an airtight window and can't actually touch the frame they are working on. This puts the cost right up.

5. **Carbon fibre.** The most common material for contemporary high-end bikes is carbon fibre. This is the lightest of all – it's now common for a road racing frame to weigh under 1kg (2.2lb). It's also possible to produce carbon-fibre tubing and lugs (the joints where tubes meet) in any shape and size, meaning areas of flex and rigidity can be built into the frame (around the bottom bracket, for instance, you need stiffness for power transmission but some flex around the chain stays and seat stays will make the bike more comfortable by soaking up bumps and vibrations coming up from the road).

    All of this construction is complicated, though: you can't produce a carbon-fibre frame in a workshop in the way that artisan builders can with steel or titanium – you need a full-scale factory to do it. If you want to enjoy the carbon experience without breaking the bank, try upgrading your forks, most of which are now routinely made from carbon fibre.

⊛ REYNOLDS 531 ⊛

Although it has been superseded in recent years by aluminium and carbon fibre, the single most successful racing component of all time is the Reynolds 531 steel tubing used in the frames of 27 Tour de France winning bikes – and innumerable others. The number is derived from the composition of elements in the steel alloy: 1.5 per cent manganese, 0.25 per cent molybdenum and 0.35 per cent carbon (other alloys offered by Reynolds included the 500, 501, 520, 525, and so on). 531 steel was also used in E-Type Jaguars.

━━━━━━━━━━━━━━━━━━━━━━

The default alloy for BMX bikes is 4130 Chromoloy

⊛ STEEL IS REAL ⊛

"Here's the way it works... [for example on] a downtube [that's] 31.8mm in diameter. The butts (tube wall thickness at the ends of the tube) are 0.9mm thick, less than a millimeter, about $^1/_{28}$th inch. To look at it, you'd think it was nothing – that the tube was on the verge of collapse. The belly of the tube (mid-portion, between the butts) is 0.6mm thick. Fortunately you can't see that, because that's even scarier. Now, in aluminium or carbon or titanium or anything other than strong CroMo steel, these dimensions would be instantly foolish and dangerous, but it works in good steel, because steel has the right balance of strength, toughness, and rigidity."

Grant Petersen (designer), on steel frames

⊛ CRACKING CARBON ⊛

If you splash out on a carbon fibre-framed bike (or one with carbon fibre componentry – many metal road bikes now come with carbon fibre forks) make sure that your second purchase is a torque wrench. Carbon fibre, compared to aluminium or steel, is brittle, and over-tensioning bolts may cause the tubing to crack. A torque wrench lets you measure exactly how much pressure you are exerting as you tighten up, letting you fit the parts securely yet without risk of material failure. There are many torque wrenches on the market – make sure you get a bike-specific one.

⊛ *VIVE LE DOMESTIQUE!* ⊛

The term *domestique* was first used by legendary Tour de France originator Henri Desgrange. Strongly opposed to any kind of co-operation, he coined it in 1911, in order to insult Maurice Brocco, a talented rider of the day (*domestique* literally means "servant"). Desgrange suspected Brocco of having paced the much weaker rider François Faber in exchange for cash – an intolerable affront to Desgrange's sense of individual heroism. An enraged Brocco accosted Desgrange at the start of the next stage and proceeded to destroy the opposition, winning the stage and taunting Desgrange throughout. Such a strong ride only made the allegations that he had deliberately thrown the previous stage all the more plausible, of course, but that did not matter.

Over the following decades, Desgrange would lose his battle against teamwork and a strong *domestique* would become a major asset for any rider wishing to win the Tour.

"You did whatever he wanted, including the fetching of beers, which he had a great fondness for in mid-race. Domestiques were reduced to chasing long miles to bring the great man a bottle of Stella."

Vin Denson (Rik van Looy's *domestique*) in
***Pro Cycling*, 2002**

⊛ FEEL THE LOVE, AUSSIE STYLE ⊛

Australian fans of the Tour Down Under, the first event in the UCI's year, have taken to randomly selecting an obscure rider – preferably an unheralded *domestique* who speaks no English and has no chance of winning – and treating him like the race's biggest star. "Operation Support Obscure TDU Pro", as this is known, involves making T-shirts, swamping his Facebook page, painting messages of support onto the road, cheering him in his own language, and requesting photos and autographs at every opportunity. This taste of the big time leaves the rider in question understandably confused, but – as Daniel Searson of the Port Adelaide Cycling Club which organizes the event points out – with "some good memories of Australia."

◉ KNIGHTS OF THE ROAD ◉

Sir Bradley Wiggins was awarded his knighthood in December 2013, a year and a half after the Tour De France triumph that presumably sealed the deal. True to form, he gave good soundbite, speaking of his feelings at meeting the other distinguished honourees; "I've won a bike race, you know, and I feel a little bit inferior to everyone, really."

Sir Francis J. Campbell (former teacher) had, by any reckoning, an eventful life. Born in 1832 and raised in Tennessee, he set his mind on music and studied in Germany before returning to the States. A staunch abolitionist, he was threatened with lynching for teaching African-American slaves to read and subsequently moved to London, where he taught music and pursued not only cycling but other outdoor pursuits such as football and mountaineering until his death in 1914. His achievements were made all the more amazing by the fact that he had lost his sight at the age of four and was completely blind.

Sir Alan Sugar (businessman) has three top-of the range Pinarello machines (one for each of his homes). He rides twice a week and credits the hobby with reducing his weight by several stone.

Sir Frank Bowden (aristocrat and businessman), 1st Baronet of the city of Nottingham, was another knight who took up cycling for the sake of his health. Given six months to live at the age of 38, he started riding and liked his bicycle so much that in 1887, he bought the business that had made it – Messrs Woodhead, Angois & Ellis of Raleigh St., Nottingham. Within six years the renamed Raleigh company was the world's largest bike manufacturer; Bowden enjoyed its success for many years, defying his doctor's prediction and living to the age of 73.

Sir Chris Hoy (track cyclist), the most successful Scottish Olympian of all time, was inspired to take up cycling by Steven Spielberg's movie *E.T.*

Sir Hubert Opperman (politician), an Australian racer, was the first professional cyclist to be awarded a knighthood – although this was in recognition of his later political career, rather than his considerable achievements in cycle sport. He completed the Tour de France in 1928 and 1931, coming 18th and 12th, broke British records by the score and won the Paris–Brest–Paris race in 1931 (riding 1,168km/726 miles through terrible conditions in a record-breaking 49hr 23min).

Another notable win was the Bol D'Or 24-Hour Classic, a paced event at a Paris velodrome: he delighted the huge crowd by winning on a substitute machine after two of his own had been sabotaged and then continued for an extra 79 minutes in order to break the 1,000km (620-mile) speed record. Achieving great fame in France (a Montmartre *gendarme* once held up the traffic for all except him and waved him through with the benediction, *"Bonjour, bonne chance, Oppy!"*) and Australia, he continued to ride until his 90th birthday, at which point his wife Mavys persuaded him to stop.

Sir George Young (politician) was for many years the most prominent champion of the bicycle in British politics. Elected to Parliament as the Member for the west London constituency of Acton in 1974, he regularly cycled from there to Parliament at impressive speeds. Despite being a member of a very car-oriented Conservative government, he actively promoted cycling, lobbying British Rail to make it easier to get bikes onto trains – and earning himself the soubriquet "The Bicycling Baronet" in the process.

Sir Arthur Conan Doyle (author) was an enthusiastic tricyclist and conceived many of his stories while out on a two-seater with his wife.

Sir Paul Smith (menswear designer) was a member of Beeston Road Club as a boy and had no ambitions apart from cycle racing. A serious accident hospitalised him for several months at the age of 17; in hospital he met some students, which eventually led him into tailoring, and then fashion design. Today there are stores bearing his name worldwide – and he continues to support cycle racing, too.

◉ THE BICYCLE AND JAMES JOYCE ◉

On 16 June 1904, the day Irish writer James Joyce chose to set his epic novel *Ulysses*, the bicycle would have been a common sight on the streets of Dublin. This is reflected in their repeated appearance in the text: there are two dozen instances of the word "bicycle" or its derivations.

In the story, Molly Bloom is irritated by her husband Leopold ogling "Those brazenfaced things on the bicycles with their skirts blowing up to their navels" (she herself would have been a fan of the knickerbocker, it would seem). Joyce himself once rode 56km (35 miles) from Galway to Oughterard to see for the first time the cemetery which he had already described in his epochal short story, *The Dead*. To his delight, he found a grave there marked "J. Joyce".

⊛ THE BICYCLE AND SAMUEL BECKETT ⊛

Nobel-prize winning Irish author Samuel Beckett was a keen cyclist in his youth and the bike is a motif in many of his novels – notably, *Molloy*, *Mercier and Camier* and *More Pricks than Kicks* – used to explore ideas of mobility, freedom and personality.

His most famous work features no bicycles, but does have a connection in its title. At some point in the late 1940s, Beckett came across some Parisian youths hanging around outside the famous Vélodrome d'Hiver. When asked what they were doing, they replied that they were waiting for the star racer, Roger Godeau – in French, *on attend Godeau*. This became the title of the famous Beckett work, *En Attendant Godot* (in English, *Waiting for Godot*).

––––––––––––––––––

"The bicycle is a great good. But it can turn nasty, if ill employed."

Samuel Beckett (author and Nobel Laureate) in *Mercier and Camier*

⊛ THE BICYCLE AND FLANN O'BRIEN ⊛

Author Brian O'Nolan, who wrote under the pseudonym Flann O'Brien, did not in his lifetime receive the international recognition of Joyce or Beckett, although he is today seen by many as a pioneer of post-modern literature.

Bikes play a prominent role in *The Third Policeman*, a novel which remained unpublished until after O'Nolan's death in 1966. In particular, the comic figure of Sergeant Pluck comes up with "an atomic theory of the bicycle" according to which he, like Beckett, perceives an interdependence between rider and ridden:

"People who spend most of their lives riding iron bicycles... get their personalities mixed up with the personalities of the bicycle as a result of interchanging of the atoms of each of them and you would be surprised at the number of people in these parts who nearly are half people and half bicycles."

⚙ TYRE TYPES ⚙

There are two tyre designs. Most tyres are "clinchers". These are the standard U-shaped tyres that hook onto the wheel rim, with an separate inner tube that pumps up underneath. Pro road racers use specialist "tubular" tyres (or "tubs"). As the names suggests, the tyre is constructed as a tube, with the inner tube hidden inside. Tubular tyres are glued onto special rims.

⚙ MATURED TYRES ⚙

Until well into the modern era, the rubber used in racing tyres was somewhat unstable and prone to puncture. Pro racers their stored tubular tyres (see above) for a couple of years before use, allowing the rubber to cure and become more puncture resistant. One notable victim of this problem was the Hercules team entered into the 1955 Tour de France. Contracted to Dunlop, who supplied the team with freshly-made "tubs" they suffered, according to rider Brian Robinson, "more than our share of punctures and other troubles." He was, despite that, the first British rider ever to complete the Tour, coming a creditable 29th in the General Classification. His compatriot Tony Hoar was that year's *Lanterne Rouge* (the wooden spoon).

⚙ PUNCTURES ⚙

You get more punctures in the wet than the dry: rainwater lubricates both rubber and nasty sharp objects, making it easier for the latter to penetrate the former.

⚙ PUNCTURE SPOTTING ⚙

Pump the inner tube then hold it under water – the puncture will appear as a tell-tale stream of bubbles. Early riders in the Australian Outback, where water can be scarce, blew tobacco smoke into a punctured tube to see where it emerged.

"Nothing hisses quite so sweetly as a rival's puncture."

Tim Krabbé (author) in *The Rider*

⊛ FIXING A PUNCTURE ⊛

If you're travelling any distance, don't forget to pack either a
puncture repair kit or a spare inner tube and don't rush the repair,
should disaster strike. Follow this checklist:

1. Once you've found the hole in the tube, double-check for
   another nearby (if it's a pinch flat, there can be two holes) and
   also make sure you can identify what caused it.
2. Run a finger gently round the inside of the tyre to locate the
   point of the intruding object before replacing it.
3. If you can't find the offending object, check the rim of your
   wheel to make sure that the problem isn't caused by the end of
   a spoke poking through the rim tape.

Two if-all-else-fails temporary puncture fixes, for when you don't
have a repair kit or inner tube to hand, are:

1. Take out the inner tube, stuff the tyre with as much grass or foliage
   as you can cram in, replace the tyre and very carefully ride on.
2. Holding the inner tube at the point where it's punctured, tie a loop
   in it and pull it tight (be warned – this is easier said than done).
   Stretch the tube over the rim, replace the tyre, re-inflate and very
   gently ride on. But this technique won't work for mountain bike or
   other smaller-diameter wheels, or if you have a very narrow tyre.
   Both of these fixes will leave your handling very compromised
   so proceed with extreme caution and make a proper fix as soon
   as you can.

⊛ SOCIALISTS ⊛

The National Clarion Cycling Club was formed in 1895 with the
aim of promoting "Cyclists for Mutual Aid, Good Fellowship and the
Propagation of the Principles of Socialism, along with the Social P
leasures of Cycling".

Members of the Club and its many affiliates would use their bicycles
to distribute leaflets and socialist literature. Although this has now
ceased to be the main focus of activity, the Clarion CC exists to this
day and, with several hundred members, is one of the country's larger
cycling social clubs.

"The bicycle is a vehicle for revolution. It can destroy the tyranny of the automobile as effectively as the printing press brought down despots of flesh and blood."

Daniel Behrman (author) in *The Man Who Loved Bicycles*

✹ CARSON BUTLER ✹

Carson Butler, star forward of the Dallas Mavericks basketball team, has donated more than 2,500 bicycles to young people in the city of Racine, Wisconsin, where he grew up. Having endured a difficult childhood (he was arrested 15 times on weapon and drug charges before he turned 15), he asks recipients to "sign a peace pledge, swear to ride safely, and be a pillar of the community."

✹ PUBLIC BICYCLES ✹

A sign that we might be now entering a new golden age of cycling is the proliferation of municipal bike-sharing schemes. After a few false starts, these are spreading widely – London, Paris, Bordeaux, Minneapolis, Washington DC, Melbourne and many other cities now boast successful schemes, and that list is ever-expanding. Rides taken on the public bikes can now be counted in the many millions per year.

The bikes themselves (made by several companies around the world – the Montreal-based firm DeVinci are one) have many special features that make this possible. Brakes and gears are sealed in wheel hubs, protecting them from theft and the elements; custom-made components cannot be transferred to other bikes as the nuts and bolts don't have standard heads; tyres are inflated with pure nitrogen, which requires less re-inflation than air. Gear ratios are deliberately low and tyres are fat and heavy, which makes the bicycles comfortable for short, low-speed journeys around town, but unglamorous and undesirable for thieves. The luggage carriers are open-sided, which means they don't get used as litter bins, and brake and gear cables are hidden safely away inside the aluminium frames.

This attention to detail has made these machines some of the most important bikes currently in production – despite the fact that they're slow, heavy, expensive, inflexible and no individual cyclist actually owns one (or would want to!).

⊛ THE WHITE BICYCLES OF AMSTERDAM ⊛

The ancestor of today's free bicycle schemes was the Dutch
White Bicycle plan devised by the gloriously-named Luud
Schimmelpenninck in 1965. Schimmelpenninck was a member
of the Provo anarchist group, a collection of radical thinkers who
sought to provoke the Dutch establishment and suggested radical
new ways of living. Their July 1965 pamphlet, *Provocation No.5,*
explained the solution to the problems of pollution and congestion
in the centre of Amsterdam. Fifty bicycles, painted white, were
distributed unlocked around the town, free for anyone to use. As
leaving an unlocked bicycle was a criminal offence, the police swiftly
cracked down on the scheme: the Provos responded by attaching a
combination lock to each machine and painting the lock's code onto
the frame.

In the face of this state opposition, the scheme did not take off,
but two years later Schimmelpennink was elected to Amsterdam's
Municipal Council, where he proposed that the scheme be rolled out
at the rate of 20,000 new bikes per annum. Unsurprisingly, this was
voted down, but it was an idea that refused to die and the public
bicycles that have now proliferated across northern Europe are
known in Dutch as *witte fietsen* (white bikes) to this day.

⊛ LONDON'S PUBLIC BIKES ⊛

It was not entirely surprising that within a couple of months of the
"Boris Bike" scheme (nicknamed after London Mayor Boris Johnson)
launching in London, informal races were being organised around
the city. Formats ape those of professional racing: there's the
mass-start head-to-head race (which has taken place in Regent's
Park), the "time trial" in which racers choose their own route
between designated bike stands (and use the system's database to
authenticate their results) and the *contre la montre* – race against
the clock – in which riders simply go as far as they can in a given
period (again using official data to determine who wins).

The appeal is threefold: firstly, the bikes are all the same, so
it's a pure test of athleticism and street knowledge; secondly,
it's plainly a ludicrous (and fun) pursuit, as the bikes are too
heavy – and geared too low – to get up any kind of speed; thirdly,
since racing is forbidden by the terms and conditions of use, it's
glamorously illicit...

⊛ GHOST BIKES ⊛

"Ghost Bikes" is the name given to the white-painted bicycles, with attached memorial plaques, that have appeared at crash sites in recent years. Intended both to commemorate cyclists that have been killed in collisions with traffic and to draw attention to cyclists' vulnerability to motor vehicles, they have drawn praise from victims' families, especially in the US, where the practice originated. The first was placed in St Louis, Missouri, in 2003: to date, the website *www.ghostbikes.org* records the locations of ghost bikes in more than 20 countries worldwide.

⊛ CYCLISTS' WAR MEMORIAL ⊛

A monument to those British servicemen who died while in service on bikes stands on the green at Meriden in the West Midlands. Dedicated in 1921 "To the Lasting Memory of those cyclists who died in the Great War 1914–1918", it is a 9m (30ft) high granite and concrete column. In the decades after the war, thousands attended the annual memorial services held there.

⊛ THE RIDE OF SILENCE ⊛

The third Wednesday of every May sees cyclists around the world (and especially in the US) take to the roads to commemorate fallen riders. The aims are similar to Critical Mass (to pay respect to the victims of accidents, to raise awareness of cyclists and to press for roads to be shared), but the atmosphere is very different. The rides are completed at a sombre pace – the maximum speed is 20km/h (12mph) – and, of course, are silent.

⊛ WHITE WEDDING ⊛

White bikes needn't necessarily be memorials. After Beyoncé's sister Solange Knowles wed Alan Ferguson in a celebrity-stuffed New Orleans ceremony, the happy couple proceeded to the reception on bright white bicycles, decorated with white roses. Aww! Romantic! The happy couple's joy in the moment was reportedly undimmed by the fact that the groom suffered a puncture, which he did not stop to repair.

◉ A CHRONOLOGY OF BRAKES ◉

Understandably, the first concern of bicycle designers has always been making a machine that moves quickly. However, as anyone who's found themselves in a situation where they need to stop suddenly, straightaway, without fail, brakes are every bit as important. Here's how the technology has developed over time:

1816   The earliest brakes – and one still in everyday use today, when all else fails – are the rider's **feet**, pressed firmly to the ground. Useful when riding bikes such as the *draisenne* (hobby-horse) and the "safety bicycle" (both of which were low enough for a rider's feet to touch the ground), but unfortunately impossible for riders of "Ordinary" bicycles (penny-farthings) who were only able to slow down by applying pressure to their spinning pedals and consequently lived in fear of steep descents.

1868   Pickering & Davis bicycles had a **brake block** fitted to the back of the saddle, which was movable. The speeding rider would push on the handlebars to force the saddle back, pressing the block onto the (iron-rimmed) wheel.

1868   A later technology featured a **hook**, mounted behind the back wheel, which could be dropped into the ground: the hope being that, like a ship's anchor, it would plough into the road surface. It tended to work either extremely abruptly or not at all and was useless on a tarmac or concrete road surface.

1880s   Safety bicycles and tricycles of the era were fitted with **plunger** or **spoon** brakes. Handles (similar to today's in appearance) would force a brake block down onto the top of the front wheel. Force was applied not via a cable but levers and rods. A major disadvantage here was that the brake block (or "spoon") could force debris into the tyre, so when pneumatic tyres were introduced they could cause punctures and in the wet they were also near-useless.

1887   The **calliper brake** was patented by Browett and Harrison. This applied a rubber brake pad to the rear wheel of "ordinary" bikes (later called the penny-farthing), and was the ancestor of today's calliper brakes.

1890s   Riders on the rough trails of the Australian Outback would carry a **branch,** which could be pushed against the ground to slow them down.

1897 The **Duck Roller Brake** was patented by the magnificently named Abram W. Duck of Oakland, California. This used a lever and rod to apply two rubber rollers to the front tyre and unlike the Spoon brake, did not cause punctures. It was used by many top riders of the day.

1898 The first **coaster brake** was introduced. Mounted inside the rear wheel hub and actuated by back-pedalling, these were the most effective brakes yet and for many decades, most American bicycles employed one.

1904 The Bowden cable was introduced by Raleigh and went into mass production in connection with different varieties of **rim brake**. For the following century, it was standard equipment in Britain and Europe (although not in China, where domestic models use ineffective **lever and rod** systems to this day). Bowden cables are principally used to actuate **calliper brakes** (used on many road bikes with narrower wheel rims) and **cantilever brakes** (used on mountain bikes and others with wider wheel rims).

1930 The **delta brake** was invented. Clean and attractive to look at, it was not as powerful as **cantilever brakes** (which it slightly resembled) or **calliper brakes** and despite being in production with Campagnolo as late as the 1980s, the **delta brake** was never widely adopted.

1982 The **roller cam** brake was invented by Charlie Cunningham. Offering sensitivity and power, it was appealing to mountain bike riders. Requiring regular maintenance and complicating wheel changes, it never achieved universal popularity though.

1990s The first hub-mounted **disc brakes** were introduced and rapidly found favour with mountain bikers. An adaptation of auto and motorcycle brakes, they are powerful, easy to keep clean and offer sensitive control. The disadvantages are that they are heavy, more difficult to service and require strong mountings to the stays and forks. As the braking torque is transmitted through the spokes, the front wheel also needs to be cross laced and extremely strong. Despite these requirements, the braking advantages and power of the **disc brake** have rendered **rim brakes** of all kinds obsolete in competitive mountain biking and have found their way onto cyclo-cross and commuting bikes.

⊙ OVER THE BARS? ⊙

It is apparently a myth that heavy braking on your front wheel when you're going fast can cause the bike to somersault. It does, however, feel a lot like that when hard braking brings your bike to a rapid halt as your momentum tries to send you over the handlebars. To avoid this feeling when braking hard on the front wheel, brace your body firmly against the handlebars and shift your body weight backward off the rear of your saddle.

⊙ BRAKE FROM THE FRONT ⊙

Your front brake is much more effective than your rear one because when you decelerate, your body weight presses against the handlebars and transmits force down the forks, pressing the front wheel hard against the ground, thereby increasing friction. Simultaneously, your rear brake becomes less effective; weight moves away from the back wheel, decreasing friction between the tyre and the road surface. In general, if your front brake is working well and the weather's dry, you don't need your rear one. But the rear brake comes into its own in the wet, when skidding is more likely (a front-wheel skid normally means a wipe-out, while a rear-wheel skid is more easily managed) and when you've got a long downhill sequence, when the rear brake can be used to shave off speed.

⊙ LEFT HAND FRONT BRAKE. RIGHT? ⊙

In the UK and Europe it is a legal requirement for the front brake to be operated by the right hand while the rear brake, which is less effective at providing stopping power, is operated by the left. This is not the case in the USA and other parts of the world, where the usual rule is for the rear brake to be operated by the right hand if local traffic drives on the right, and the left hand, if local traffic drives on the left – confused? There is no clear consensus as to why this is: what is certain is that if you borrow a bike abroad, you should double-check how the brakes are set up before riding off.

Never use your face as a brake pad.

Jake Watson (mountain bike racer)

⊕ BOWDEN CABLES ⊕

When you pull on your brakes, the force is transmitted to the blocks along a Bowden cable. Launched in 1896, this cable was the invention of Ernest Monnington Bowden and came to replace heavy and cumbersome lever systems as a means of transmitting force around the bike's componentry.

Their invention is often wrongly attributed to Ernest's namesake, Sir Frank Bowden, owner of the Raleigh bicycle company, which adopted the system in 1902. The two men were not related.

⊕ THE HUB DYNAMO ⊕

Invented in the 1930s, the hub dynamo is a tiny power-plant mounted inside the front wheel hub. As the wheel turns, the dynamo generates enough electricity to power a pair of bike lights. As they reduce the wheel's efficiency and create some drag that the rider must overcome, they have never been universally popular but in recent years, advances in technology have seen them become more efficient and lighter. They are fitted to the bikes of the London Cycle Hire Scheme, for instance, powering their distinctive LED light units.

⊕ THE BOTTLE DYNAMO ⊕

Simpler cousin to the hub dynamo, the bottle dynamo is mounted so that a roller is rotated by the rim of the bicycle. Like hub dynamos, they do add drag but have the advantage that they can be disengaged altogether when not in use.

A modern variant, the Pedal & Power unit (manufactured by Ikon), allows you to charge your mobile phone (or any other low-power unit) while pedalling.

⊕ PEDAL POWER ⊕

The "safety bicycle" (the forerunner of today's bike design, using a chain-driven rear wheel) swiftly became an important form of transport for bushmen and prospectors in rural Australia. One company marketed an accessory that allowed a stationary bicycle to power a hand-held sheep-shearing device.

⊛ THE EMBACHER COLLECTION ⊛

Guaranteed to make any bike-lover sick with envy, the collection
of Austrian architect Michael Embacher comprises around 200
bicycles of all kinds, from high-performance carbon racing models to
limited-run prototypes, classic steel racing bikes and unsuccessful
folding machines. No fewer than eight Moultons are included; also
featured is an ice-bicycle, with a skate mounted to the front forks
in place of a front wheel and a metal-studded rear tyre. Highlights
are often exhibited in public and there is an excellent website (*www.
sammlung-embacher.at*) documenting his machines.

⊛ THE DUNWICH DYNAMO ⊛

One of the most distinctive of the world's mass cycle rides is the
annual Dunwich Dynamo run from Hackney in east London to
Dunwich, a village on the Suffolk coast. The 193km (120-mile)
run takes place overnight (hence the name) on the Saturday in
July closest to the full moon. The first ride, organised by bike
messengers riding fixed-wheel machines, took place in 1993 and
the ride has been steadily attracting more entrants ever since.
Around 1,000 – including at least one penny-farthing rider – now
take part, relishing the ride's uncompetitive nature, the beautiful
sight of the bunch's lights passing through rural darkness, and the
promise of an early-morning dip in the sea at the end.

⊛ LONDON TO BRIGHTON ⊛

Europe's largest mass-participation bike ride is the annual London–
Brighton run, which attracts in excess of 30,000 participants each
year. Since 1980 it has been run in association with the British
Heart Foundation, which claims to have raised more than £40m
($65m) for its research and treatment programmes.

⊛ THE ARGUS ⊛

The largest competitively-timed bike race in the world is South Africa's
Cape Argus Cycle Race. Up to 31,000 compete – not all seriously
– and the event is recognized by the UCI. Run in early March, it is
vulnerable to the variable weather of the Cape and has, in previous
years, been cancelled due to both strong wind and extreme heat.

◉ THE NAKED BIKE RIDE ◉

The first Naked Bike ride took place in 2001, in Zaragoza, Spain. Conceived as a colourful protest against "Indecent Exposure to Cars", rides now take place in about 70 cities worldwide, with naked, nearly-naked, body-painted and simply underdressed cyclists baring their bodies in defiance of local decency laws. Typically the events attract hundreds of riders: the smallest seems to have taken place in Newcastle, Australia, in 2005, when only five riders turned out.

◉ SANCTIONS BUSTERS ◉

J. Burns, G. Main, D. Nixon, P. Nugent and A. Owen were the bland pseudonyms chosen by a group of young Irish and British riders who wanted to race in 1975's Rapport Tour. So, why the subterfuge? The event was in South Africa, then in the grip of apartheid, and subject therefore to an international sporting boycott.

An alert journalist, John Hartdegen of the *Daily Mail* (who was in South Africa covering the second honeymoon of Elizabeth Taylor and Richard Burton) realized something was up and sent photos of the mystery riders back to London for identification. The names that came back included one that would go on to become one of the most distinguished in cycling's history. A. Owen was none other than a young (and at the time, still amateur) Sean Kelly (later a top-class pro racer). Hartdegen promptly exposed the racers.

Although only initially banned from competition for a few months, the riders then received lifetime bans from Olympic competition as a result of their sanctions-busting mischief; the Rapport Tour had been planned as an important part of their preparation for the 1976 Games in Montreal.

Kelly went on to win a host of classics and major stage races. One of his team-mates, Pat McQuaid ("P. Nugent") went into administering the sport after his retirement: he is currently president of the UCI (cycling's world governing body) and in early 2010, was elected as a member of the International Olympic Committee, which puts him in the interesting position of organizing the very events from which he himself has been barred for life.

⊛ CRITERIUM INTERNATIONAL ⊛

The Criterium International is a two-day stage race run in March: it's the successor to the *Criterium National*, which was open only to French riders but was thrown open to international riders in 1979. The most distinctive racer, however, was a brown horse which in 1997 jumped out of its paddock and galloped into the middle of the peloton near Toulouse. The alarmed riders swiftly slowed down and let the horse canter on ahead, which it did to great applause.

Louison Bobet, who won the Tour de France in 1953, 1954 and 1955, was forced off his bike after his last triumph by a terrible saddle sore that required surgery. He used the time off to learn how to pilot a plane and would fly between post-Tour criteriums in order to minimize travelling time.

⊛ THE DEVIL ⊛

Arguably road racing's most recognisable fan, the German Dieter "Didi" Senft has become one of the characteristic sights of the Tour de France and other European stage races. Sporting a red devil's outfit (complete with horns, tail and trident), a black cloak and a magnificent white beard, he lurks at the side of the course and urges the riders on with diabolic glee. In common with many Tour fans, he also paints on the road surface: a trident will appear some miles before his chosen spot, giving the riders (and an increasingly interested media) some warning of his appearance.

He is also credited with having created a number of novelty bicycle designs, perhaps the most impressive being the world's biggest mobile bike-guitar. Recognized by the *Guinness World of Records*, it is over 14m long and 4m high, and was built from more than 300m of aluminium piping and 40m² of corrugated aluminium sheeting, with stainless-steel strings. It weighs more than half a ton. Understandably, it is not a bike that can be ridden that often.

But that's not the end of his eccentric creativity. Other, equally impractical designs include the world's longest bike (38m long), a mobile Eiffel Tower and the awesome "Kicker-Velo", which is nearly 3m high and 6m long, with enormous tyres made from 61 full-sized footballs.

⊛ COMPUTERS ⊛

The first speedometers and odometers for bikes date back to the late 19th century but it was not until 1981 that Tom Boyer became the first pro racer to use a cyclo-computer on the Tour de France.

⊛ FRONT WHEEL FURTHER ⊛

A bicycle's front wheel travels further than its rear one. This is because the slight steering movements that are necessary to keep machine and rider balanced cause it to steer from side to side in a wavy path. Your back wheel also does this, but the arcs are smaller so the total distance travelled is less.

⊛ CRITERIUMS ⊛

Criteriums (city-centre races) were a major source of income for racing pros. After finishing the Tour de France, they would shuttle about the country again, collecting appearance fees at these smaller races, which were usually set up to be won by local heroes. Jean Stablinski (who rode as a *domestique* for both Jacques Anquetil and Raymond Poulidor) once rode 48 "crits" in the 42 days *after* completing a 5,000km (3,000-mile) Tour de France.

⊛ NOTABLE MEN'S HOUR RECORDS ⊛ (CONVENTIONAL BIKE)

The challenge of riding as far as possible in one hour in a velodrome has been cycling's most prestigious record for well over a century and the motivating force behind some of high-speed cycling's most important technical innovations – including aerodynamic helmets, disc wheels and monocoque frames. In order to make the record reflect human endeavour rather than technical or aerodynamic innovation, the UCI has strictly regulated the kind of machines and positions which are permissible (including all of the innovations just mentioned and Graeme Obree's "praying mantis" riding position).

Overleaf is a listing of how the record has been raised over time. If Frank Dodd's initial record seems a good deal more modest than that of Henri Desgrange, bear in mind that unlike all the later riders he accomplished the feat on a penny-farthing.

Date	By	Location	Distance (km)
1876	Frank Dodds		26.508
11 May 1893	Henri Desgrange	Paris	35.325
31 October 1894	Jules Dubois	Paris	38.220
30 July 1897	Oscar Van Den Eynde	Paris	39.240
3 July 1898	Willie Hamilton	Colorado Springs	40.781
24 August 1905	Lucien Petit-Breton	Paris	41.110
20 June 1907	Marcel Berthet	Paris	41.520
22 August 1912	Oscar Egg	Paris	42.122
7 August 1913	Marcel Berthet	Paris	42.741
21 August 1913	Oscar Egg	Paris	43.525
20 September 1913	Marcel Berthet	Paris	43.775
18 August 1914	Oscar Egg	Paris	44.247
25 August 1933	Jan Van Hout	Roermond	44.588
28 September 1933	Maurice Richard	Sint-Truiden	44.777
31 October 1935	Giuseppe Olmo	Milan	45.090
14 October 1936	Maurice Richard	Milan	45.325
29 September 1937	Frans Slaats	Milan	45.485
3 November 1937	Maurice Archambaud	Milan	45.767
7 November 1942	Fausto Coppi	Milan	45.798
29 June 1956	Jacques Anquetil	Milan	46.159
19 September 1956	Ercole Baldini	Milan	46.394
18 September 1957	Roger Rivière	Milan	46.923
23 September 1959	Roger Rivière	Milan	47.347
30 October 1967	Ferdi Bracke	Rome	48.093
10 October 1968	Ole Ritter	Mexico City	48.653
25 October 1972	Eddy Merckx	Mexico City	49.431
27 October 2000	Chris Boardman	Manchester	49.441
19 July 2005	Ondrej Sosenka	Moscow	49.700
18 September 2014	Jens Voigt	Grenchen, Switzerland	51.110
30 October 2014	Matthias Brändle	Aigle, Switzerland	51.852
8 February 2015	Rohan Dennis	Grenchen, Switzerland	52.491
2 May 2015	Alex Dowsett	Manchester	52.937
7 June 2015	Sir Bradley Wiggins	London	54.526

"The velocipede is one step ahead on the road taken by the genius of Man. In place of collective speed – which is brutal and unthinking – it offers individualised speed: rapidity founded on the power of reason. It is able to circumvent obstacles, adapt to conditions, and is subject to the will of the rider."

Richard Lesclide (journalist) in *Vélocipède Illustré*, 1861

"I'm not going for stage wins, just the 'most elegant rider' and 'most unfortunate rider's' prizes."

Tom Simpson (former pro cyclist), Tour de France, 1967

◉ NOTABLE WOMEN'S HOUR RECORDS ◉

In the women's record, Jeannie Longo-Ciprelli dominates, breaking the record six times between 1986 and 2000:

UCI Hour Record

43.501km/h Anna Wilson-Millward (AUS), October 2000
44.767km/h Jeannie Longo-Ciprelli (FRA), November 2000
45.094km/h Jeannie Longo-Ciprelli (FRA), December 2000
46.065km/h Leontien Zijlaard-Van Moorsel (NED), October 2003

UCI Best Hour Performance

41.347km/h Elsy Jacobs (LUX), November 1958
41.471km/h Maria Cressari (ITA), November 1972
43.082km/h Keetie van Oosten-Hage (NED), September 1978
44.770km/h Jeannie Longo-Ciprelli (FRA), September 1986
44.933km/h Jeannie Longo-Ciprelli (FRA), September 1987
46.352km/h Jeannie Longo-Ciprelli (FRA), October 1989
48.159km/h Jeannie Longo-Ciprelli (FRA), October 1996
47.112km/h Cathérine Marsal (FRA), April 1995
47.411km/h Yvonne McGregor (GBR), June 1995

◉ LEONARDO'S INVENTION? ◉

The announcement in 1974 of the discovery of a sketch of a bicycle on one of Leonardo da Vinci's manuscripts unsurprisingly caused something of a stir in bicycle-mad Italy. Was it possible that the great man had come up with the concept of the bike – complete with pedals and rear-wheel chain drive – some 400 years before anyone else? Supporting evidence, including diagrams elsewhere of chainwheels and power transmissions, and the fact that he undoubtedly devised many machines of greater complexity, seemed to argue that he had invented the bike. Literary historian Augusto Marinoni, who had worked extensively on Leonardo's manuscripts, put da Vinci forward as the bicycle's creator. Against him were ranged the sceptics, led by his colleague Ladislao Reti, who pointed out that the crude drawing was clearly not from Leonardo's own hand, that parts of the sketch did not seem to date from the same era as the (mostly pornographic) sketches that surrounded it, and – crucially – that the drawing was too similar to a modern machine. Reti summarized his view as: "This is really a bicycle – therefore it is a forgery!"

To explain the sketch's poor draughtsmanship, Marinoni suggested that it had been drawn by one Gian Giacomo Caprotti da Oreno, a badly-behaved young apprentice who had entered Leonardo's household in the year 1490 and who, despite many fallings-out with da Vinci, stayed there for years. The theory was that he might have crudely copied a since-lost design of his master's; Reti, though, rejected this outright, accusing Marinoni of having manipulated a genuine fragment (of two circles, with mudguard-like semi-circles above) while working on the documents in the 1960s. In the absence of a confession from Marinoni or one of his colleagues, no one knows exactly what happened, but his claims are now rejected by the vast majority of Leonardo scholars.

And what became of the unruly apprentice Gian Giacomo? He died in 1525, some six years after his master, and among his effects was a small but intriguing painting on wood: the portrait of a Florentine silk merchant's wife that is today known as the *Mona Lisa*.

"In Italy, the bicycle belongs to the national art heritage in the same way as [the] Mona Lisa by Leonardo, the dome of St. Peter or the Divine Comedy. It is surprising that it has not been invented by Botticelli, Michelangelo, or Raffael."

Curzio Malaparte (Italian author), 1949

⊙ FACT AND FICTION ⊙

So many myths and inaccuracies have grown up around the history of cycling that a British historian, Derek Roberts, was commissioned to write an entire book debunking them and setting the record straight. *Cycling History – Myths and Queries* was published in 1991. It has proved invaluable to historians ever since. Roberts was awarded an MBE for services to cycling.

⊙ NOTABLE HOUR RECORDS ⊙
(HUMAN-POWERED VEHICLE – RECUMBENTS)

Recumbent bicycles, where the rider is almost lying down, have a huge advantage over conventional racing models, sustaining only a fraction of the wind resistance that is the fast rider's main obstacle. In

1933 this was demonstrated unambiguously by Francis Fauré, a racer who had an undistinguished record on conventional bikes but sped a recumbent to a record distance of over 45km (28 miles) in one hour, breaking Oscar Egg's world record, which had stood for 19 years.

Outraged cycle manufacturers, sensing this would detract from their models and lose them business, lobbied the sport's governing body, the UCI, into ruling the result invalid and on April Fool's Day 1934, the UCI published a new specification (including the position of the bottom bracket relative to the ground, the saddle and the front wheel) that bicycles would have to meet to be considered for the record in future.

Undaunted, fans of the recumbent formed their own ruling bodies (the International Human Powered Vehicle Association and the World Recumbent Racing Association) and since then have wheeled their machines ever faster and farther – beating conventional bikes over the same distance by a huge margin. The Canadian Sam Whittingham, who designs and builds high-speed recumbents, holds world records in several events.

Date	By	Location	Distance (km)
7 July 1933	Francis Faure	Paris, France	45.055
18 November 1933	Marcel Berthet	France	49.99
1938	Francois Faure	France	50.53
5 May 1979	Ron Skarin	Ontario, California, USA	51.31
4 May 1980	Eric Edwards	Ontario, California, USA	59.45
4 May 1980	Ron Skarin & Eric Hollander*	Ontario, California, USA	74.51
29 September 1984	Fred Markham	Indianapolis, USA	60.35
10 September 1985	Richard Crane	Warwickshire, England	66.30
28 August 1986	Fred Markham	Vancouver, Canada	67.01
15 September 1989	Fred Markham	Adrian, USA	73.00
8 September 1990	Pat Kinch	Bedfordshire, England	75.57
27 July 1996	Lars Teutenberg	Munich, Germany	78.04
29 July 1998	Sam Whittingham	Blainville, Canada	79.136
7 August 1999	Lars Teutenberg	Dudenhofen, Germany	81.158
27 July 2002	Lars Teutenberg	Dudenhofen, Germany	82.60
19 November 2003	Sam Whittingham	Uvalde, Texas, USA	83.71
31 July 2004	Sam Whittingham	Dudenhofen, Germany	84.215
2 July 2006	Fred Markham	Casa Grande, Arizona, USA	85.991
8 April 2007	Sam Whittingham	Casa Grande, Arizona, USA	86.752
12 July 2008	Damjan Zabovnik	Lausitzring, Germany	87.123
19 July 2009	Sam Whittingham	Ford Michigan Proving Grounds, USA	90.598
2 August 2011	Francesco Russo	Lausitzring, Germany	91.556

⊕ THE FASTEST RECUMBENT ⊕

Official speed records for recumbents are governed by the rules of
the International Human Powered Vehicle Association. A number
of records are recognized, the fastest of which is the "flying 200",
a distance of 200m (656ft) on level ground from a flying start with
a maximum allowable tailwind of 1.66m/s. The current record is
132.47km/h (82.33mph), set by Sam Whittingham of Canada in a
fully faired Varna Diablo front-wheel-drive recumbent low-racer bicycle
designed by George Georgiev.

⊕ RECUMBENT OR CONVENTIONAL BIKE? ⊕

It's commonly claimed that the bicycle is the most efficient form of
travel – or even machine – ever invented. This is true if you're talking
about recumbents. As noted in the previous story, by lowering the rider
and putting him or her in a near-horizontal position, wind resistance
is significantly reduced, enabling faster speeds. Devotees of the
recumbent ride also point to their stability, comfort and safety; the
only significant downside seems to be riding uphill, which is a slow
business as you cannot deploy your body weight to help you drive down
on the cranks.

⊕ WORD UP ⊕

In December 2010, *Cycle Sport* magazine published a list of the 50
greatest books ever written about cycling. Forty-nine of them were
non-fiction of one kind or another; the exception being Tim Krabbé's
The Rider (which came in at number six). Foreign writers were only
represented by six titles, women (as subjects or authors) by none,
and there was a strong bias toward tales of the Tour de France.
Despite that, the list provides a useful introduction to the genre
and contains many classic reads. Here are the top five:

1. *Wide-Eyed & Legless* by Jeff Connor
2. *A Rough Ride* by Paul Kimmage
3. *Kings of the Road* by Robin Magowan
4. *Lance Armstrong's War* by Dan Coyle
5. *Kelly: A Biography of Sean Kelly* by David Walsh

(The complete list may be seen on *Cycle Sport's* website.)

⊛ ONE MAN LIBRARY ⊛

Tim Dawson manages the website www.cycling-books.com, which aims to review and catalogue every book about the subject in English and consequently offers a wealth of ideas if you're stuck for something to read.

⊛ CYCLING AND THE CHURCH ⊛

The French surrealist writer Alfred Jarry (1873–1907) was a passionate wheeler, who scandalized turn-of-the-century Paris by wearing a racing cyclist's outfit at every opportunity and often sped around town with a pair of revolvers tucked into his belt, a rifle strapped to his back and the loud bell from a tram on his handlebars. (After Jarry's death, one of the revolvers fell into the hands of Pablo Picasso.) Author of the revolutionary play *Ubu Roi*, he incorporated the imagery of cycling into much of his work. Undoubtedly his most famous cycling piece is the scandalous *Passion Considered as an Uphill Cycle Race*. Published in April 1903, it blasphemously retells the events leading up to Christ's Crucifixion in a parody of the breathless sports journalism of the time, complete with mock-academic references to obscure Dutch philosophers of the late Renaissance.

"You have no idea what the Tour de France is. It's a Calvary. Worse than that, because the road to the Cross has only 14 stations and ours has 15. We suffer from the start to the end."

Henri Pélissier (Tour de France winner), 1923

⊛ MADONNA DEL GHISALLO ⊛

Pope Pius XII responded to an appeal from an Italian priest and recognized the Madonna del Ghisallo as the patron saint of cyclists. The Madonna had been seen by a local nobleman as a vision on a hillside overlooking Lake Como in northern Italy and for hundreds of years, there has been a chapel dedicated to her on the site. The fact that this chapel was handily located for a climb that frequently featured in the *Giro di Lombardia* was a happy accident and Madonna del Ghisallo swiftly became a shrine to deceased cyclists and to cycle sport itself. Today it is packed with images of racers and memorabilia, and is a destination for thousands of riders per year.

Near the chapel and carved into the very hillside is a museum of cycling with some quite incredible machines on display: Italian army machines dating back to the early years of the 20th century and racers ridden by such names as Coppi, Merckx, Moser, Rominger and Bartali. There is also a copy of *L'Auto* from 1903, announcing the beginning of the very first Tour de France.

◉ REPACK RACES ◉

Madonna del Ghisallo is perhaps the holiest mountain for road racers, but mountain bikers will pick another hill. Called "Repack", west of the town of Fairfax in Marin County, California, this was where the first downhill mountain bike race was held, on 21 October 1976. Starting from a lookout point on the eastern side of Pine Mountain, with views over the hills and San Francisco Bay, the 3.4km (2.1-mile) course descends 400m (1,300ft), with numerous technical corners, hazards and tricky surfaces. The bikes were not what we would today recognise as mountain bikes, but "cruisers", some 30 years old, stripped down and fitted with performance components.

The record time was held by Gary Fisher, who completed the course in 4min 22sec, but the most successful racer was probably Joe Breeze, who won 10 of the time trial events. Both – along with many other Repack regulars – went on to distinguished and continuing, careers in bike design and manufacture. The last official race down the course was held in 1984.

The route gained its unusual name from the fact that after a couple of runs, the bearings in their hubs would have become so hot that the grease would burn off. The hubs would then need a fresh application ("repacking") of grease.

"I'd lunge forward, driving all my weight on the pedals to produce enough momentum to help me muscle the tall gear over a slight rise 50 yards out. From there it was all downhill and speed. The road is littered with in-line gullies, blind and off-camber turns, and the occasional cluster of head-size rocks. Knowing the road beyond each

turn was key. I had made mental notes of landmarks such
as geology, flora, and past mistakes. Among the latter
were Danger X and Breeze Tree (whose moniker wasn't
earned as harshly as Vendetti's Face). The course
rolls quickly down the ridge to the steep final face,
which has a series of four switchbacks.
These steep sharp turns, especially Camera Corner,
would be lined with spectators. Then it's a final
straightaway; another blind turn, across the finish
line, and into a big Franz Klammer slide."

Joe Breeze (mountain bike pioneer) on riding Repack

⊕ THE US BICYCLING HALL OF FAME ⊕

For over 20 years, the United States Bicycling Hall of Fame has been
honouring that nation's greatest cyclists and celebrating the sport
and art of cycling. It now honours over 100 figures from cycling's
golden age to the present: early inductees included legendary
figures like early champions Major Taylor, Frank Louis Kramer and
Arthur Zimmerman, plus many fascinating items of memorabilia
and machinery. These include bicycles that belonged to Kramer and
Taylor alongside *draisiennes*, unicycles and a large collection
of modern bikes. The Hall of Fame is located in Davis, California,
north-east of San Francisco.

⊕ THE *LAUFSMACHINE* OF BARON VON DRAIS, PLUS OTHERS ⊕

The first commercial entrepreneur of the velocipede was probably
Baron Karl von Drais, a member of the German minor nobility, who in
1817 invented a two-wheel wooden running-machine as an alternative
to the horse. Although propelled by the rider's feet kicking along the
ground, it could be steered and the rider balanced the machine in
the same way as cyclists today do. By the standards of the time it
was amazingly fast: far quicker than horse-drawn vehicles on a good
surface, although not so good on bad roads or in the wet.

By 1818, von Drais had patented the design and launched
it commercially in Paris, where his machine was christened the
draisienne. After a disastrous start (a demonstration event was ruined

by children chasing the rider), *draisenne*-riding caught on and the machines became staples of Paris's amusement parks.

Despite his patents, von Drais's simple design was widely copied and imitations of his machine were soon seen throughout Europe. London carriage-maker Denis Johnson improved the design, incorporating an iron frame, and opened two riding schools, where fashionable young Englishmen (including royalty) grew confident enough to start racing each other and horse-drawn vehicles, too. (The first London to Brighton ride took place in 1819: a "hobby-horse" rider beat a coach by half an hour.) By the end of the year, in response to the growing number of accidents the first restrictions on velocipedes had been enacted and riding on London's pavements was punishable by a fine of £2 ($3) in old money.

The craze spread to the USA, where the *draisenne's* design was re-named the "Tracena" and smartly re-patented by the Baltimore musical instrument maker, James Stewart: he sold them at $8 (£5) each to the sportsmen of Philadelphia. New York was quickly overtaken by the first of several cycle crazes. By the end of the year, American riders too were being fined for sidewalk-riding – $3 (£2).

Sadly, the early velocipede's impracticalities and the poor state of the roads at the time prevented it from establishing itself in the long term. Nowhere did the velocipede craze last longer than a year and only a few creative mechanics continued developing the invention in isolation. And as for the pioneering Baron von Drais? Frustrated by commercial failure, he turned to drink, was suspected of insanity, lost his title and finally died, in poverty, in 1851.

⊚ HOBBY-HORSES RUN RIOT ⊚

"...running at the rate of ten knots an hour, he capsized a Dandy, a Member of Parliament, a Pig, an Apple-woman, a Cabinet Minister, a Prince, a Newfoundland Dog, and a Bishop. The rapidity with which all this was executed, proves that, under the guidance of discretion, these Hobby-Horses may be made very useful in accelerating every wise and nobler art of man."

John Fairburn (newspaper proprietor, educator and politician) describes a rider in *The New Pedestrian Carriage*, 1819

⊛ HOBBY-HORSE VERSE ⊛

"Vain was the brief boneshakers' ride
They had no go-it, and they died.
In vain they seemed, inane they fled.
They made no poet, and are dead."

Joseph Grinnell Dalton (poet) in *The Harp of Rota*, 1880

⊛ NAPOLEON RIDES ON ⊛

The young Napoléon Prince Imperial of France (1856–79), son of Emperor Napoléon III, was such a keen wheeler that he was known in Paris as "Vélocipède IV".

••••••••••••••••••••••••••••••

A century later, the French pro racer Henry Anglade was known to the peloton as "Napoléon". He was bossy, he had good tactical sense – and he was short.

⊛ EDUCATED TOWNS ⊛

Davis, California, is a small town with the bold motto "Most bicycle-friendly town in the world". Residents enjoy the full range of cycle-friendly developments and a high rate of journeys taken by bike. It is perhaps no coincidence that it is the second most educated city in the United States, with just under 35 per cent of the population in possession of a graduate degree.

⊛ POTHOLE FIXER ⊛

Potholes can swallow your front wheel and send you flying. Report them using "Fill That Hole" at *www.fillthathole.org.uk*. (They also have a smart phone app, allowing you to file your report on location.) Whether or not you're a member, the CTC (Cycle Touring Club) will identify the responsible authority and contact them on your behalf; they claim an impressive clear-up rate.

According to their data, the most efficient pothole-filling authorities are: Cheshire West and Chester, Redbridge, Luton, Cumbria and Norwich. Bottom of their league table is Shetland.

◉ BIKE LANE PIONEERS ◉

The world's first bike path was constructed in California in 1897. Running between the cities of Pasadena and Los Angeles, it was a toll route; for 15c you had the right to ride a smooth pine surface, electrically lit, free of pedestrians, motors and horses. Surviving photos show an elegant raised structure snaking through the suburbs and over the Los Angeles river. Sadly, it was not a financial success and, falling into disrepair, was torn down within a decade. The US's first freeway, the Arroyo Seco Parkway, now follows the route.

◉ BIKE LANE BLUES ◉

One of the most common irritations of urban cycling is the illegally-parked motor vehicle blocking a bike lane. Why not express your frustration at them by taking a photo and uploading it to *mybikelane.com*? This international site allows users to plot the locations and licence plates of obstructive vehicles. Police vehicles are, apparently, among the worst offenders and the site has been used to embarrass police forces into "encouraging" their officers to be more considerate.

"You haven't lived until you've put on a police uniform and hopped on a mountain bike. My daily commute became four to five minutes faster because drivers fight each other to see who gets to let me into the lane I want. Drivers would sooner cross the yellow line and hit a utility pole than breeze a cop on a bike. I've completed centuries and even won races, but this newfound respect is the sweetest cycling experience of all."

Allan Howard (police officer and cycle safety expert)

◉ COLLISIONS ◉

One of the founders of the CTC was Frederick Bidlake. Although he had unreconstructed views of women riders (he viewed races for women as "undesirable" and female competitors as "dishevelled, grimy and graceless"), he did a great deal to establish time trialling in the UK; a heritage which many years later has contributed to the UK's remarkable modern success in track racing and time trials. Bidlake died after colliding with a car in 1937 at the age of 66; a public subscription in his memory raised so much that an award in his name is still given to this day. The Bidlake Memorial Prize has since been awarded annually to distinguished riders (including female racers like Beryl Burton and Nicole Cooke) and supporters of cycling alike.

"Newspapers are unable, seemingly, to discriminate between a bicycle accident and the collapse of civilization."

George Bernard Shaw (author and Nobel Laureate)

⊛ USEFUL INVENTIONS ⊛

Hubs with ball-bearings were invented in France in 1869 – just as the front-wheel drive velocipede craze was at its height. Invented by Jules Suriray, they were manufactured by convicts (Suriray was the Superintendent of Prisoner' Workshops in Paris). They quickly proved their practical worth, as the winner of the first Paris–Rouen race – the Englishman James Moore – used them later that year, but the 1870 War with Prussia interrupted production and the French initiative was lost to British manufacturers.

The Wright Brothers, Orville and Wilbur, did not manufacture bikes in quantity, but they did come up with an innovation in 1897 which is in universal use today. They were the first mechanics to machine the threads of the left-side crankarm and pedal in the opposite direction to normal. Prior to that every revolution of the crank had exerted a small loosening force on the pedal on that side: to this day, left side pedals have a left-hand thread and are consequently held securely by the rider's natural motion. One of their bicycles is on display in the National Museum of the US Air Force at Dayton, Ohio.

"Business is like riding a bicycle. Either you keep moving or you fall down."

Frank Lloyd Wright (bicycle engineer and aviator)

⊛ PATENT OVERFLOW ⊛

Such was the outpouring of mechanical ingenuity in the early years of the bicycle that by 1900 the U.S. Patent Office required two buildings to hold its records in Washington, DC. One building was reserved for bicycle patents, the other was for everything else.

⊛ BIKE FIT ⊛

The two key measurements relating to bike fit are the distances from pedal to saddle and from saddle to handlebar. It's worth making a note of, or memorizing, these two distances.

Measure the first from the centre of the crank axle (or bottom bracket) to the top of the saddle (via the seat tube) and the second from the same point on the saddle to the centre of the handlebars. Knowing these two figures allows you to quickly configure a new or borrowed bike to be as comfortable as possible.

"Few people realize that when you move the seatpost an innocent inch or two you are changing the action of every muscle in the lower limb which is involved in the pedalling action."

Professor Peter R. Cavanagh (expert on biomechanics)

⊛ SPOKE PATTERNS ⊛

Rear wheels have tangentially spoked wheels (in which the spokes cross over each other, usually two or three times) because they need to transmit torque (driving and braking power) from the hub to the rim. (Picture the rotating hub hauling the rim after it.) Front wheels, on the other hand, can be radially spoked (a simpler arrangement in which the spokes do not cross, but radiate outward like slices in a cake). This results in a stiffer, lighter wheel but one that does not transmit power well. Braking systems that act on the hub (particularly the powerful disc brakes which now appear on many mountain bikes) also demand tangentially-spoked wheels.

Unlike the wooden spokes of cartwheels, bicycle wheels are held together by tension. This means that – counter-intuitively – the rider's weight is not borne to the ground by the spoke, which is pointing straight downward, but instead "hangs" from the spokes pointing upward. The weight then passes through the wheel-rim to the ground.

"[Bicycle] wheels surely count among the greatest of human inventions."

David Gordon Wilson (scientist) in *Bicycling Science*

⊛ INVENTION OF THE SPOKE ⊛

The radially-spoked wheel was invented by the Frenchman Eugene Meyer in 1869: the tangentially-spoked wheel, devised by the prolific English innovator James Starley, followed soon after.

"A thin hoop of extruded aluminium is laced to a hub with a handful of steel spokes that exert a collective force of several tons. A pair of these structures can support up to 500 times their weight, sustain repeated pounding from the road or trail, endure substantial side loads during cornering, and transmit pedalling and braking torque. All this while remaining true to within a fraction of a millimetre."

Doug Roosa (author), on the strength of the bicycle wheel

"It is by riding a bicycle that you learn the contours of a country best, since you have to sweat up the hills and coast down them. Thus you remember them as they actually are, while in a motor car only a high hill impresses you, and you have no such accurate remembrance of country you have driven through as you gain by riding a bicycle."

Ernest Hemingway (author and Nobel Laureate) in *By-Line*

⊛ TYRE TRACKS ⊛

A tyre was produced in 1930s Germany that left a print of a swastika in the dirt behind it.

⊛ SHERLOCK'S ON YOUR TAIL ⊛

The great detective Sherlock Holmes came across a few cyclists in the course of his adventures and was able to differentiate between the tracks of no fewer than 42 tyres.

⊛ POET'S CHOICE ⊛

"The bicycle, the bicycle surely, should always be the vehicle of novelists and poets."

Christopher Morley (author and journalist)

⊛ EARLY VERSE ⊛

To the best of our knowledge, the first poem to mention a velocipede was John Atkin's *Jonah Tink* of 1819, a long ballad about a rural dandy. The hero, Jonah, is proud of his machine and imagines that it will impress the ladies:

> That he might faster on proceed,
> He rode on a *velocipede*.
> Well knowing that upon the way
> It wanted neither corn nor hay;
> He fancied that when he alighted,
> Into the house should be invited;
> That lovely Susan would be kind,
> And he a good reception find.

⊛ SILLY VERSE ⊛

Appearing many years later, in the era of the high-wheeler, the first volume of poetry about cycling was *Lyra Bicyclica*. This light-hearted anthology was edited by Joseph Grinnell Dalton of Cambridge, Massachusetts, and was published in 1880. The poems included were parodies, dubious in quality, of the work of Longfellow, Wordsworth, Byron, Shakespeare and many more. Of little artistic merit, they do nevertheless capture the heady enthusiasm of the time – and some of the dangers of high-wheeling on bad roads:

> Going leg after leg
> (As the dog went to Dover)
> When he came to a stone
> Down he went over.

Published a few years later in New York, *Wheel Songs* by S. Conant Foster was a more artistically successful collection, although it shared a concern with the perils of uneven terrain and its potential disasterous consequences:

> He went for a peaceable roll;
> His wheel took a piece of a hole,
> And it soon came to pass
> That a requiem mass
> Was sung for the peace of his soul.

An anonymous contemporary of Mr Foster's identified a phenomenon of bike buying that most of us will still recognize (remember, at the time it was common to call a bike a "wheel"). His experience of the costs involved is as true today as it was in 1896…

> Hey diddle, diddle
> The bicycle riddle
> The strangest part of the deal
> Just keep your accounts
> And add the amounts
> The "sundries" cost more than the wheel.

The bicycle has made frequent appearances in verse ever since, with varying degrees of artistic success. A final word on the subject from John Betjeman:

> I think that I should rather like
> To be the saddle of a bike.

⊛ OLD-SCHOOL ATTITUDES ⊛

In the late 19th century, the Cyclist's Touring Club insisted that members who rode on a Sunday covered up their club badges.

"Being born into a poor family, that was my strength. If you're brought up without frills and you know what hunger is, it makes you hard enough to withstand bike races."

Karel van Wijnendaele, founder of the Tour of Flanders

⊛ SELF-SABOTAGE ⊛

Well into the post-war period, riders of the Tour de France were subject to a bevy of inconvenient regulations. One was the rule that punctured tyres had to be replaced onto the same rim: simply swapping the whole wheel for one with a fresh tyre already mounted was not allowed. Riders circumvented this by deliberately damaging the spokes or rim of a punctured wheel, ensuring that a whole new wheel was needed and no valuable time was lost on replacing a tyre.

⊛ IRRESISTIBLE ⊛

"I love the bicycle. I always have. I can think of no sincere, decent human being, male or female, young or old, saintly or sinful, who can resist the bicycle."

William Saroyan (dramatist)

⊛ THOUGHTS ON MAINTENANCE AND CARE ⊛

"The learner, having acquired the art of riding his new steed, his affection for and pride in it will prompt him to take care of it. It is said that a good horseman is known by the care he takes of his horse; and this is in some sense true of a bicycler: a good rider will not use a machine in bad condition. The first requisite is that the bearings be properly oiled..."

Charles Pratt (lawyer and cycling advocate) in
***The American Bicycler*, 1879**

☉ RUNNING SMOOTHLY ☉

*"Be at one with the universe. If you can't do that,
at least be at one with your bike."*

Lennard Zinn (bike builder, author and former pro cyclist)

"A loved bike is a quiet bike."

Matt Seaton (author and journalist)

----

*"When your bike functions best, you don't hear it – it's
silent, there's no cracking, just shhhh – you're gliding.
It's the same when you're in good shape and you're in
form and you're riding your bike, you hear nothing –
maybe just a little bit of breath."*

Ralf Hütter (musician and member of Kraftwerk)

----

*"A bad machine carefully kept, may, perhaps, last longer
than a good machine very badly managed. It should be
the ambition of a good rider, however, to have a good
machine, kept in good order."*

**J.T. Goddard (author and advocate) in *The Velocipede: Its History,
Varieties and Practice*, 1869**

----

*"Cleaning a bike's like cleaning a toilet. If you do it regularly, it's fine
and easy. If you wait, it's a truly disgusting experience."*

Steve Gravenites (pro mechanic and wheel engineer)

----

*"If the bicycle could speak, it would have much to say,
presented ever so quietly and unobtrusively."*

James E. Starrs (author) in *The Literary Cyclist*

☻ THE PLASTIC BIKE ☻

The Itera was the world's first plastic-framed bike. Launched
in Sweden in 1982, this box-framed beige roadster was a
commercial failure: the bikes were supplied in kits for self-
assembly, but they were frequently incomplete and it also proved
hard to replace broken parts. After three years the company
behind them gave up, exporting the remnants of their stock to
the West Indies, where – being impervious to rust – they were
surprisingly popular.

☻ A LAYMAN'S GUIDE TO ENERGY ☻

The chemical reactions that power your muscles rely on six
different fuels – two fast-acting compounds, three carbohydrates,
and one fat. Here's a (very) simplified breakdown of how and when
they work to move you along.

1. **Adenosine triphosphate**, or ATP, is the only fuel directly used
    by your body's muscle fibres. It can be metabolized without
    oxygen (anaerobic), and the only waste product is heat. Each
    resting muscle fibre holds enough ATP for about two to five
    seconds of all-out effort and it's about 50 per cent efficient –
    half of the energy stored can be turned into useful work, the
    other half is lost as waste heat.
2. **Phosphocreatine,** or PCr, steps in when the ATP runs out.
    It can be metabolized very quickly to form ATP, without
    oxygen. The ATP then runs the muscles. Your muscles hold
    enough PCr to work for about 10 seconds – approximately
    the length of the final phase of a bunch sprint finish in
    a race.
3. **Glucose** (a simple sugar), **glycogen** (a related starchy
    compound, which stores tens of thousands of glucose
    molecules) and **lactate** (partially-metabolised glucose) are
    carbohydrates. When the muscle has run out of stored ATP
    and PCr, it will rely on glucose in the blood or glycogen
    stored in the muscle tissue, which can be metabolised
    into ATP.

    When there is ample oxygen (aerobic), this process
    is relatively efficient. But if there is not enough oxygen
    (anaerobic), the sugars are not completely metabolized, and

leave behind lactate. This inhibits the work of the muscle fibre and is what makes them hurt – very quickly, if you're working at high power levels; slowly, if your effort is more steady and the blood is able to carry oxygen to your muscles and ferry some of the lactate away. (This lactate isn't wasted, however – your liver will eventually turn it back to glucose.)

So, the anaerobic process is much less efficient than the aerobic process and is only 7 per cent efficient, meaning that your muscles generate great heat as well as huge quantities of painful lactate. The glycogen stored in your muscles may well keep them going for a couple of hours aerobically, but will be burned up anaerobically in a matter of minutes.

4. **Fat**. Because fat contains oxygen, it metabolizes extremely efficiently – but it cannot be carried easily round the blood (unlike glucose) or sit patiently until needed within the muscle (unlike glycogen). This means that it tends to be depleted more by low-to-moderate exercise for prolonged periods than short, high-intensity bursts.

What does this mean for the cyclist?

1. Don't work anaerobically for more than a few seconds early in a ride. You'll be giving lactate build-up a head start and wasting the glycogen stores in your muscles.

2. Exercizing aerobically, your muscles are carrying enough glycogen for a couple of hours.

3. After that point, you'll need to run on glucose and you should refuel by eating some. Running out of both glycogen and glucose causes the energy crisis that riders know as the "bonk".

4. Your brain needs to be working, too – and not being a muscle, stores no glycogen and can only use glucose.

5. The best way to work off fat is to ride for a long time, at low intensity, often.

6. The worst situation to be in is hot, low on water, high on lactate, low on glycogen and glucose, and struggling for oxygen. This is why Henri Desgrange, the organizer of the first Tour de France, was called an "assassin" by the second rider to make it over the 1,700m (5,600ft) high Col d'Aubisque in 1910. A competitive, high-altitude climb in summertime, after several hours spent working in the saddle and building up lactate, is a recipe for pain.

7. If you can arrange a massage after such a strenuous day, do so – it will shift the lactates out of your legs and relieve the pain. But if you can't, try a recovery ride, spinning your legs at a rapid cadence but in a low, easy gear. This will help to flush lactates back into the bloodstream, where they can be carried away.

⊛ EATING HABITS ⊛

Attitudes to nutrition have always varied amoung pro riders: Jacques Anquetil was famous for heavy indulgence in rich cuisine and alcohol the night before (and even the morning of) a race. Tom Simpson, on the other hand, travelled everywhere with a book about fruit and vegetable nutrition, and in the off-season drank a litre of fresh carrot juice every day. Tom Boyer, the first American Tour de France rider, was a vegetarian, known for the amount of nuts and fruit he would consume while racing; Sean Yates ate anti-social quantities of garlic; track racer Graeme Obree famously relied on white toast and marmalade, and would travel with a carton of skimmed milk and some cornflakes just in case there wasn't anything to eat when he arrived. Today's riders frequently complain about the monotony of their breakfasts – large portions of energy-giving pasta.

"I took rice cakes and rice pudding, apples, sliced-up bananas, plus calcium, and I put a lot of glucose in my drinks."

Vin Denson (former pro cyclist) quoted in *Sex, Lies and Handbar Tape*

☺ CALORIE CONSUMPTION ☺

The amount of kilocalories burned by cycling obviously varies according to your weight, your route and how fast you go. Speed is the biggest factor in affecting how many you burn. In general, at 16–24km/h (10–15mph), you'll burn off extra kilocalories in the low hundreds per hour. At 24–32km/h (15–20mph), this figure roughly doubles. And if you can ride for an hour at 40km/h (25mph), you can expect to get through over a 1,000.

A pro cyclist on one of the Grand Tours will consume about three times as many calories (about 7,500) as a normal person would need (about 2,500) on every day of the race – and still lose weight over the course of it.

The first British team to race in the Giro d'Italia was the Linda McCartney Racing team. Sponsored by Linda McCartney's eponymous vegetarian food business, the team was not a long-term success and broke up in 2001 after three years' racing. It was managed by Sean Yates, and Bradley Wiggins was a member for a brief time: both are currently with Team Sky.

☺ CULTURE SHOCK ☺

"My first time there was daunting. The guy who met us at the airport stank of garlic. I didn't know what the f*** garlic was in 1983 and this waft came off this bloke and made me think, 'what the f*** is going on here?' We passed by a cafe that afternoon and I saw people eating these big plates of mussels and chips. "I was looking at them, thinking 'f***ing hell, these people are barbarians'. I went to the shop and the stink of the f***ing cheese counter just blew me away. The culture shock was huge."

Paul Kimmage on moving from Ireland to France to turn pro

◉ PAIN ◉

"At any given moment, every human being has at his disposal a brief intense death struggle that doesn't hurt and which lasts 12 seconds. That's the animal sprint."

Tim Krabbé (author) in *The Rider*

"The thing I like to do is not think of it as 'pain', but as 'that feeling I get when I'm riding correctly'. Do that long enough and you'll actually start to believe it."

Mark Hickey (bicycle maker)

"To be a cyclist is to be a student of pain... at cycling's core lies pain, hard and bitter as the pit inside a juicy peach. It doesn't matter if you're sprinting for an Olympic medal, a town sign, a trailhead, or the rest stop with the homemade brownies. If you never confront pain, you're missing the essence of the sport. Without pain, there's no adversity. Without adversity, no challenge. Without challenge, no improvement. No improvement, no sense of accomplishment and no deep-down joy. Might as well be playing Tiddly-Winks."

Scott Martin (author and amateur racer)

In French, a bad day on the road is known as a *jour sans* – literally, "a day without". The "bonk" (where a rider runs out of energy) is known as *la fringale*.

◉ FAKING IT ◉

If your main rival in a race appears conspicuously out-of-sorts, temper your sympathy with suspicion. Many is the pro, from Simpson to Cavendish, who has faked a bad day in the saddle before surprising the opposition with a strong finish "out of nowhere". By the same token, a racer who is really having a bad day will try to hide the fact.

⊛ MOUNTAINEERING ⊛

"I climb cols [mountains] by feel and I don't look at my heart meter. That said, I do have a look at my rivals' heart meters sometimes, to see what state they're in."

Richard Virenque (seven-time Tour de France King of the Mountains), 2002

••••••••••••••••••••••••

"One night, when I was dropping off to sleep, I started thinking about how lovely it would be if some reporter suddenly got cramp in his fingers in the middle of writing his article about me, but he couldn't just stop. He had to go on, tapping away at his typewriter with his agonising cramped fingers, just as we have to ride on. If they went through that, I think some critics might write differently about us, when we're in trouble in the mountains."

José Manuel Fuente (three-time Giro d'Italia King of the Mountains)

⊛ HYDRATION ⊛

The importance of hydration was not properly appreciated until the 1970s. Racers were not allowed to accept water from the team cars (in case they held onto the car to steal a lift) so were limited to the two *bidons* (500ml bottles) of water that they could carry on their bike and two more that were passed in their *musette* (feed bag) halfway through the day. Thirsty riders would raid cafés, bars and fountains *en masse*. These days, it is estimated that the riders of the Tour de France get through about 15,000 plastic bottles.

••••••••••••••••••••••••

"It was so hot that the tar was melting under our tyres. I was completely dehydrated. I ended up stopping beside a farm and I lapped up the dirty water from a cattle trough. And that's how I got foot-and-mouth disease. It's usually only cows that get that!"

Raphaël Géminiani (Tour de France stage winner)

⊛ SAFETY IN TRAFFIC ⊛

As all of us know, cycling in traffic can still be an intimidating experience. Here are some statistically verified ways to encourage other road users to treat you with respect.

1. Don't ride in the gutter in the belief that you should avoid traffic there. Not only does this expose you to the broken glass and other rubbish that will punish your tyres, it puts you more at risk of collision with pedestrians – and it actually *decreases* the leeway that passing cars will grant you. A study by Cycle Training UK (an independent training body) shows that passing drivers note how far into the roadway a cyclist is, then pass them with the same clearance.

2. Pass parked cars by at least a door's width; watch for movement inside the car and faces in the wing-mirrors, which may give you an early warning of a door opening in your path.

3. Check behind you frequently. It not only tells you what's approaching, it also makes the rest of the traffic more alert and responsive to your presence.

4. Communicate with the traffic – hand signals and head movements. Be predictable.

5. Make eye contact with drivers, ahead and behind alike.

6. When large vehicles are stopped at lights, never pull up beside them. A high proportion of fatal accidents are caused by trucks and similar large vehicles moving off and colliding with cyclists, which their drivers haven't seen. Stay well behind or, where practical, well in front.

7. Don't listen to music on headphones: remain fully aware of your environment using all your senses.

8. Wear highly visible clothing so you can be easily seen.

There may be 10 million bicycles in Beijing, but that unfortunately doesn't make it a safe city to cycle around. Car usage is expanding exponentially, and it is estimated that up to one third of drivers on the city's roads don't possess a licence. According to official figures, something like 10,000 cyclists are injured on the city's roads every year and 1,000 are killed: similar figures nationwide make China far and away the most dangerous nation to cycle around.

◉ TERRIBLE NOISES ◉

"The sound of a car door opening in front of you is similar to the sound of a gun being cocked."

Amy Webster (musician), on one of the perils of riding on the roads

◉ THE GOLDEN BOOK OF CYCLING ◉

The nearest thing Britain has to the US Bicycling Hall of Fame is probably the "Golden Book of Cycling", a collection of illuminated calligraphic manuscripts dedicated to distinguished riders and influential figures. It was compiled between 1932 and 1972 (the first and last entries were dedicated to Frank Southall and Hugh Porter, respectively) by the editors of *Cycling* magazine.

At that point, the original volume was full of racers, administrators and inventors. Nearly 20 years later, the Pedal Club resurrected the tradition and since then has maintained a second "Golden Book" with nominees voted in by its (strictly limited, and exclusively male) membership.

◉ RUSH HOUR ◉

In the late seventies, only 4,000 people regularly commuted into work in central London. Thirty years later, this number had risen by a factor of more than 20 and the Cycling Revolution London plan (backed by the London Assembly, the Mayor's Office and a collection of other bodies) aims to double the figure again by 2026.

◉ THE GOLDEN BIKE ◉

Established in 1999, the UCI Golden Bike is an international series of Sportive cycling races. The lofty aim of the events (all of which would take place without the UCI's recognition) is to "unite cycling amateurs from around the world".

The current events include the Sportives on the following page, most of which offer a selection of routes depending on how arduous a day's ride you require:

1. Cape Argus Pick n Pay Cycle Tour (Cape Town, South Africa)
   A 106km (66-mile) circuit taking in Africa's southernmost point, starting and finishing in Cape Town. In 1985 it was won by a tandem.

2. Lake Taupo Cycle Challenge (Taupo, New Zealand)
   A 160km (100-mile) lap of Lake Taupo, a volcanic caldera in the middle of New Zealand's North Island. First run in 1977 with only 26 riders, the event now attracts many thousands and has turned Taupo into a major destination for cyclists year-round.

3. De Ronde van Vlaanderen (Belgium)
   The tourist version of the "Monument" of the same name run the day before over the same course. You don't have to complete the full 260km (162 miles) of the main event, but the cobbles and weather are every bit as unforgiving as those the pros will face.

4. Gran Fondo Internazionale Felice Gimondi (Bergamo, Italy)
   Named after the great Italian racer, this has a number of climbs, even if you opt for the shorter course. Participants may chose to pay homage to the greats of Cycling's golden era by wearing one of the event's official woollen jerseys.

5. Quebrantahuesos (Spain)
   Perhaps the most difficult of the Sportives listed here, "La Quebranta" is not only 205km (127 miles) long, but takes in several tough climbs and the variable weather of the Pyrenees in June. Recommended only for the fit.

6. Cyclosportive l'Ariégeoise (France)
   Billing itself as one of the world's most beautiful Sportives, this 179km (111-mile) tour of the Pyrenees features five hefty climbs, including the second-category Port de Lers.

7. Gruyère Cycling Tour (Switzerland)
   Despite its beautiful alpine setting between Lausanne and Bern, this is probably the least challenging of the European Golden Bicycle events.

⊛ THE KILO ⊛

The shortest of the major distance records in cycling is the kilometre or "Kilo". Only three times has this distance been ridden in under one minute: twice by Sir Chris Hoy in 2007, and once by the current record-holder, the Frenchman Arnaud Tournant, in 2001. All three rides took place in La Paz, Bolivia – the Bolivian capital's velodrome is situated 3,658m (12,001ft) above sea level. It is much easier to break short (anaerobically orientated) speed records at high altitudes like this, as the lower air pressure reduces wind resistance.

The downside is that the high altitude also reduces the amount of oxygen available to the rider, which is not an issue over such a short distance but makes recovery from the all-out effort involved in cycling at such as speed "quite unpleasant", as Hoy puts it.

⊛ LONG ROAD ⊛

The Pan-American Highway runs down the West Coast of the Americas for about 22,500km (14,000 miles) through some of the world's most amazing landscapes. The current record for cycling its entire length is held by Scotsman Scott Napier, who completed the journey from Prudhoe Bay, Alaska to Ushuaia, at the southern tip of Argentina, in 125 days: an average of 180km (112 miles) a day.

This was considerably faster than the first woman to complete the journey: June Siple started in June 1972, but did not arrive till February 1975.

⊛ FIRST RIDE IN THE USA ⊛

The first cyclist in the USA was a Frenchman, Pierre Lallement: he rode a velocipede on College Green, New Haven, Connecticut in April 1866. Like so many pioneers, he was not able to take advantage of his efforts and was destined to die in obscurity in Boston in 1891, as others made fortunes from the patents he had been forced to sell.

But his name lives on: the Pierre Lallement Bike Path now runs for 5.5km (3½ miles) through South Boston and a monument to him was erected in New Haven in 1998.

⊛ THE CHAMPS-ELYSEES AND VELOCIPEDES ⊛

Paris's most famous thoroughfare, the Champs-Elysées becomes the centre of the cycling world's attention every July as the Tour de France finishes there. It's a fitting venue, for it was on the Champs that one of the most important innovations in the history of wheeling took place: in 1861, Pierre and Ernest Michaux were the first to put a velocipede with pedals into commercial production. Their wooden machines were far from perfect, but they innovated rapidly and by 1867, the latest metal-framed, rubber-tyred machines were ridden by royalty.

"Velocipedes, known in England nearly half a century ago as dandy-hobbies, occupy a vast deal of attention now in France. Manufactories are established on a large scale in Paris and elsewhere, and the new carriages, without horses, are constructed on very scientific principles, light, elegant, and with all kinds of delicate appliances, at prices varying from ten to fifteen pounds..."

"Notes" in *The Journal of the Society of the Arts*, London, Vol. 17, 1869

⊛ ON THE RUN ⊛

Until recent years, the best British cyclists were forced to move to the continent if they wanted to turn their talent into a career. Tom Simpson was no exception, but he had a pressing reason to leave in a hurry: he was avoiding National Service, which would have seen him drafted into the Army for two years. His call-up papers arrived at the family home only one day after he had moved to France and he once cancelled a trip back home having been tipped off that the Military Police were waiting for him.

⊛ PEUGEOT ⊛

One of France's best-known marques, Peugeot started manufacturing penny-farthing bikes in 1882. Prior to that their business had been in umbrellas, salt and pepper grinders, saw blades and the wire cages that supported ladies' crinolines. Ten Tour de France winners have ridden Peugeot-branded bikes.

⊛ *LE CHAMPIONNAT DES TRIPORTEURS* ⊛

The three-wheeled delivery tricycle – the *triporteur* – ridden by a young man or boy, was a ubiquitous sight on the streets of Europe for the first half of the 20th century. In 1901 the French, being cycle-race mad, started an annual race for delivery boys, *Le Championnat des Triporteurs,* in and around Paris.

As was normal at the time, the emphasis was on making the race as arduous as possible: it was around 40km (25 miles) long and each rider had to load his tricycle with 65kg (132lb) of additional weight. Many surviving photos show that the *Championnat* must have been quite a sight: the huge bikes jostled through crowds of fans, battling November weather, cobbles and Paris's sharp, steep hills.

The great Marcel Cognasson (who won the race seven times in the 1920s and 1930s) could top 60km/h (37mph) downhill and averaged nearly 30km/h (19mph) round the entire course. For the rest of the year he was a deliveryman for a printing company – but the glory of his title was considerable.

⊛ NO REGRETS ⊛

"Get a bicycle. You will not regret it, if you live."

Mark Twain (author)

⊛ FIVE CYCLING CIRCUMNAVIGATORS ⊛

More people that you might think have circled the land portions of the globe by bicycle. Here are five of the most distinguished:

1. The first widely-known circumnavigator was **Jonathan Schopp**, an American correspondent of France's *Vélocipède Illustré* magazine who rode a state-of-the-art velocipede round the world in the late 1860s, travelling at an incredible rate over difficult terrain and in defiance of hostile locals.

   As readers who attempted to follow his routes – and some did – discovered, the glamorous Mr Schopp's exploits were too good to be true. And they were; he was fictional, a light-hearted creation of the magazine's editor Richard Lesclide.

2. English-born American **Thomas Stevens** was the first man to complete a circuit of the world in reality rather than the imagination: an even more impressive feat when you consider that he did so on a penny-farthing with a 50-inch (1.3m) front wheel. He did it in three sections, sitting out winters to avoid the weather. The first leg was San Francisco to Boston (it is believed that he was the first person to complete this route), between April and August 1884. The following spring he steamed to Liverpool and, leaving in April 1885, rode from there as far as Istanbul (then known as Constantinople) before pausing, then striking out as far as Tehran in Iran, where he wintered as the Shah's guest. March 1886 saw him repulsed from Afghanistan, and he took trains and steamers as far as Madras in (then British) India. He then rode across the subcontinent, from South to North China, and through Japan before steaming home to an "enthusiastic reception" from the San Francisco Bicycle Club and the Bay City Wheelmen in January 1887.

3. The exploits of **Anne Mustoe** were proof that it is never too late to consider packing your panniers and heading off. She was 53 when she retired from her post (headmistress at a rural boarding school in Suffolk) and set off from London on her first serious ride. Her bike was a Condor tourer: in her pannier she had a copy of Horace's Odes. She completed an east-facing circumnavigation in 439 days and enjoyed it so much that she promptly headed off in the opposite direction, taking in a whole new set of countries.

   Her first book was the unassumingly-titled *A Bike Ride*. It was followed by a host of others as she recorded long-distance tours around Europe, Asia and South America – often following ancient trade routes. In 2009, she set off on another ride but after falling ill in Syria, died at the age of 76.

4. The current *Guinness World Record* holder of the fastest circumnavigation is **Alan Bate** of the UK. On 4 August 2010, he completed his circuit having taken 106 days, 10hrs and 33mins. There is no doubt that this record will be attacked in the near future, but if you are thinking of an attempt then you'd be wise to check in with the Guinness World Records people first, as the route you select has to satisfy a number

of requirements to pass muster. Meanwhile, Vin Cox plans to stage a race round the world.

5. Although the German **Heinz Stücke** has never completed a timed lap of the world unlike the above-mentioned riders, he has certainly circumnavigated the globe – many times, in fact. In November 1962 he left his hometown (Hövelhof, in north-western Germany, which he described as "small-minded") and he's never gone back. He has visited 257 countries on five continents on a three-speed bike, carrying a tent, thousands of photos and the pamphlets which he sells to support himself.

The numbers involved are mind-boggling; he's ridden something over 500,000km (311,000 miles) and taken tens of thousands of photos, worn out countless tyres and had to repair his frame many times; at one point the persistent salty drip of sweat from his nose was causing the top tube to corrode. He's been assaulted, attacked by bees and crashed into many times, but always dusts himself off and carries on, trusting in the people he meets and believing that they will also trust him. "Riding a bike," he says, "gives you the opportunity to approach people more easily. People think if you are on a bike, you cannot be a bad guy! It becomes a kind of passport, a business card."

"Somewhere in Rajasthan I looked out of the bus window and saw a cyclist, a solitary European man, pedalling across the immensity of the Great Thar Desert. I was seized with sudden envy. I wanted to be out there myself on that road on a bicycle, alone and free, feeling the reality of India, not gazing at it through a pane of glass."

Anne Mustoe (circumnavigator and author) on the moment that inspired her

---

"You don't have to be mad to go up the Ventoux, but you're mad if you go back."

Provençal proverb, on climbing the giant Mont Ventoux

◉ THE PICKWICK CLUB ◉

The oldest surviving bicycle club in the world is the Pickwick Bicycle Club, founded in Hackney, east London, in 1870. An early club achievement was member G.T. Clough's epic ride from Stratford to Norwich and back, "in 23 hours, including all stops". In the erroneous belief that Charles Dickens (who had recently died), was a keen cyclist, members of the Pickwick Cycle Club assumed the names of characters in Dickens' *Pickwick Papers*. The tradition continues to this day; there is a long waiting list for membership (places only become free on the death of a member) and the ceremonially-dressed (and one assumes, well-heeled) members assemble for annual lunches in the West End and occasional tours in the UK and France. Dickens was, in fact, a prodigious walker.

◉ THE PEDAL CLUB ◉

Meeting more regularly than the Pickwick is the Pedal Club, an association of 60 male grandees of the sport and the industry. Lunching once a month in London, they pay more serious interest to cycling's development and take pride in inviting a high quality of guest speaker to their functions.

◉ THE CYCLISTS' TOURING CLUB ◉

The Cyclists' Touring Club (for the first five years of its existence, the Bicycle Touring Club) was formed at Harrogate in 1878. Membership has fluctuated widely over the period since, first peaking at 60,449 in 1899; at that point, members still wore uniforms when out on a run (except on Sundays). In June 2009, 110 years later, that record was finally surpassed: a worthy accomplishment by an active and effective body.

◉ TEN ENGINEERING GENIUSES WHO TRANSFORMED THE MODERN BICYCLE ◉

1. **James Starley (1831–81)** Known now as the "father of the bicycle industry", James Starley was a sewing machine manufacturer who was introduced to the French bone-shaker in 1868 and was responsible for three huge innovations. For

developing the high-wheeled penny-farthing bicycle alone, his name would now be remembered, but he was also the genius behind the wire-spoked wheel that we still use to this day. Realizing the limitations of the simple radial spoke layout, he developed the tangentially-spoked wheel, allowing efficient transmission of both braking and motive force between the rim of the wheel and its hub.

2. **John Kemp Starley (1854–1901)** At the age of 18, John was sent to work at the Coventry factory of his uncle James. After some years spent mastering the construction of "Ariel" model penny-farthings, he formed his own company with a local wheelman, James Starley. In 1885, they launched the first machine with a chain drive to the rear wheel and the modern bicycle was born.

   By the time of his premature death in 1901, Starley and Sutton's "Safety" bicycles had inspired the world and their company – Rover – was one of a host producing high-quality machines to their basic pattern. After his death, sadly, the Rover company moved away from cycle manufacture; for nearly a century the name was associated with motorcycles and then cars, although the brand is now defunct.

3. **Tullio Campagnolo (1901–83)** Thanks to the company he founded, the Italian name Campagnolo is universally recognized within the cycling community. Although he was not an innovator when it came to frames or the basic geometry of the bike, he improved the quality of the other parts attached to it beyond measure. Inventing the quick-release hub in 1930, he allowed wheels to be quickly and easily replaced. In the following decade, he refined existing rear derailleur gears, making them reliable enough for race use, and introducing the "groupset" of compatible parts. This was followed by improvement after improvement, as pro racer stars such as Eddy Merckx used his equipment; in the three decades from 1968, Campagnolo components were fitted to Tour de France winning bikes 25 times.

   These innovations, filtering down to everyday bikes, are a major factor in the efficiency, comfort and flexibility of the modern bike – and *aficionados* and collectors still lust after vintage "Campag" parts to this day. The company continues under the guidance of Tullio's son, Valentino.

4. **Dr Alex Moulton (1920–2012)** Responsible for the most important reconfiguration of the upright bicycle in the modern age. Recognizing that speed and efficiency benefit from small wheels and the most rigid frame possible, he rejected the conventional frame template and worked on a series of designs which evolved into a distinctive geometric cage and high-pressure tyres with suspension systems to absorb the bumps to which the small wheels are susceptible. The bicycles look utterly distinctive, but usually out-perform larger-wheeled, conventionally-framed models in head-to-head meetings. The regulation of frame design by the sport's governing body ensures they will never be part of the mainstream circuit, but his machines (manufactured in the UK in small quantities and for sale at high prices) are works of the engineer's art.

5. **Al Fritz (1924–2013)** An American who worked for the Schwinn company for some 40 years, Fritz was not an engineering genius. He didn't accrue ingenious patents, use revolutionary materials, or have anything to do with the Tour de France. But in 1963, he took a call from a Californian salesman, who told him that youngsters were fitting long handlebars, small wheels and banana seats to their bikes in order to emulate the motorcycles ridden by California's biker gangs. The result of that call was the first low-rider bike, named the Sting-Ray. It was one of the ugliest, least-elegant bikes ever but was a huge commercial success. In the mid-1960s, 70 per cent of all bikes sold in the US were Sting-Rays or similar machines, and if you ever rode a Chopper, or a BMX, you rode one of the Stingray's direct descendants. Not the most efficient machine, but pure pleasure to glide around on.

6. **Ernesto Colnago (1932–present)** Founder of the Italian company that carries his name, Colnago has not (like Ritchie, Moulton or the Starleys) ever re-imagined the bicycle from the wheels up, or himself developed any revolutionary new technology. Rather, his art has been in the refinement and gradual improvement of the basic racing frame: small changes in frame geometry, allied with early adoption of high-quality new materials (titanium in the 1970s, carbon fibre 20 years later) and cutting-edge parts, have made Colnago a byword for fast, light, high-specification and utterly desirable road bikes. This quality is epitomized by the C40, one of the few production bikes recognised by model name alone.

7. **Mike Burrows (1943–present)** Unlike Colnago, Burrows has worked on every kind of bike but will always be best known for his part in designing the revolutionary Lotus Type 108. This was not the first bicycle to abandon a traditional tubed frame in favour of an aerodynamically efficient carbon-fibre mononcocque, but when Chris Boardman rode it on his 1992 Olympic pursuit rides, and won gold in the process, the world sat up and took notice. UCI rule changes have made the Lotus illegal, so Burrows has applied his creativity to recumbents, tricycles, folding models and heavy-duty freight carriers, as well as road bikes for Trek.

8. **Andrew Ritchie (1947–present)** Yet another Briton to re-imagine the bicycle, Ritchie has devoted his design energies to refining just one, unglamorous-sounding machine: the famous Brompton folding bike. Initially, he struggled to find backers for the design, but once he was able to start producing his distinctive bikes in 1986, they swiftly found a niche in the market and he has since won numerous awards for export and high-quality design. His bikes are all based on the same ingenious template, meaning that parts are interchangeable across the range and four ingenious folds turn the machine into an easily portable package – invaluable on Britain's bike-unfriendly trains.

9. **Gary Fisher (1950–present)** was a mountain bike pioneer, the fastest ever to ride the legendary Repack course, whose first innovations involved the modification of a 1930s Schwinn Elcelsior cruiser with parts from motorbikes and second-hand "junkers". In 1979, inspired by interest in the Repack scene, Fisher started MountainBikes, the first commercial mountain bike manufacturer. In their first year, they sold 160 machines and since then, Fisher has stayed involved, developing bikes under his name with various manufacturers and developing talent in the sport.

10. **Mike Sinyard (1950–present)** Others had come up with the idea and built a few by hand, but Sinyard was the designer of the first mass-produced mountain bike, the Specialized Stumpjumper. Launched in 1981, this was a hybrid of BMX, road bike and motorcycle elements, and was marketed as "the bike for all reasons". It was a major commercial success, and can be seen as the ancestor of the vast majority of mountain bikes sold today (which will never see a mountain) but will give their urban users a comfortable, stable ride that can withstand the worst city streets. Specialized still sell bikes with the Stumpjumper name.

⊛ FIRST SUPERSTAR ⊛

Cycling's first international superstar was the American Arthur Zimmerman. By 1894 he was reportedly earning $40,000 per year in appearance fees and prize money: something like $1m (£650,000) at today's prices – a staggering amount. He dominated the first World Sprint championships (held in 1893), winning two out of three events, and won the vast majority of races he entered.

⊛ THOUGHTS ON BIKE BALANCE ⊛

"In the history of humanity, does it not constitute the first successful effort of intelligent life to triumph over the laws of weights?"

Henri Desgrange (founder of the Tour de France) on the invention of the bicycle

"We involuntarily ask, How is it possible for one supported on so narrow a base to keep his seat so securely and, seemingly, so without effort?"

Charles B. Warring (scientist) in "What Keeps the Bicycler Upright?", *Popular Science*, April 1891

⊛ LOOK MUM, NO HANDS! ⊛

Riding no hands isn't quite so clever as it looks: the bike does most of the work. It takes a good deal of physics to explain why, but it is true that a well-designed and made bicycle will be self-righting – that is, if moving, it will steer itself and remain balanced. Depending on the design of the bike, a speed of 10–20km/h (6–12mph) should do the trick.

A bike in this ghostly, self-riding state will also tend to steady itself if knocked. The faster it goes, the more stable it will be – until the point (usually at much higher speeds) at which frame vibrations hit the right frequency for "shimmy" to kick in, making the bike unstable.

⊕ BEWARE THE CHOPPER ⊕

"One of the hallmarks of a successfully engineered bicycle – properly designed and manufactured – you could ride it for great distances, turning the corner and everything else without having your hands on the handlebars, because if it was properly balanced you just shifted your weight and made turns... Well, with a chopper fork you didn't dare take your hands off the handlebars. I remember one of our tooling engineers came to me one evening and said, 'You know, I think you're missing the ball by not coming out with one of these chopper forks.' Now, we had a sample of one there. We had a long hallway in our offices and I said, ' Go down to the end there and ride that bike,' and he rode by me smiling, and I said, 'Now, take your hands off the handlebars, and he did a brody. He crashed right into a wall. It didn't last very long – a chopper fork was not a safe item."

Al Fritz (bicycle designer)
on Chopper-style forks

⊕ CHOPPER CHIC ⊕

"For a kid in the seventies, all you cared was that they looked cool and were brilliant for doing wheelies."

Matt Seaton (journalist) on the Chopper,
in *The Escape Artist*

⊕ STRAIGHT LINES ⊕

"A bicycle that is not perfectly symmetrical generally requires an annoying steering torque, to travel straight, or an upper body lean, when ridden with no hands."

David Gordon Wilson (academic and author) in
Bicycling Science (3rd Edition)

⊛ EXISTENTIAL DISTRACTION ⊛

*"[Jean-Paul] Sartre much preferred riding a bicycle to
walking. The monotony of walking bored him, while
the intensity of effort and the rhythm of a bicycle journey
varied constantly. He would amuse himself by sprinting
on the hills. I would become winded and fall behind him.
On level stretches, he pedalled with such indifference
that on two or three occasions he landed in the ditch."*

Simone de Beauvoir (author) in *La Force de l'Age*

⊛ LOOK MUM, NO HANDS! (AGAIN) ⊛

Next time you're at a loose end in London, drop in at Look Mum
No Hands! on Old Street. It's one of the few places in the capital
where you can get your bike repaired, drink coffee and watch
cyclesport on the big screen. It also serves as a meeting place for
cycle campaign groups and supports amateur racing.

⊛ SHIMMY ⊛

"Shimmy" is the unpleasant high-frequency vibration of your front
wheel and handlebars that sometimes occurs at high speeds.
It's not dangerous if you remain calm. Don't try to counter it by
force: instead, stand up, putting your weight in the pedals (to
increase damping of the vibrations) and slowly apply the brakes.
As your speed drops below a critical velocity, the shimmy will
cease. You should then stop and make sure that there's nothing
loose, especially luggage at the back, or around the headset.
This is a frequent cause of the worst shimmy – although some is
inevitable at a high enough speed.

⊛ BIKE TALK ⊛

The most distinguished collection of words on cycling in Britain is
the National Cycle Archive at the University of Warwick. Established
in 1990, it comprises thousands of books, periodicals and other
materials to do with cycling in Britain and holds the records of
many clubs and distinguished wheelers going well back into the
nineteenth century.

⊛ SEMANTICS ⊛

"People do not 'drive' cars, they steer them.
People do not 'ride' bicycles, they drive them."

Anon

"Is it not time we stopped riding our bikes and began
to drive them? Similarly, who ever drove a car?
We ride them. Words Matter."

Andrew Shrimpton (bike retailer and activist)

⊛ CRASH LANDING ⊛

The penny-farthing (or "high-wheel", or "ordinary ") bicycle had a
number of design flaws but the most serious was the propensity
of the machine to throw its rider off on encountering a bump in the
road. Enterprising designers came up with a variety of solutions,
including detachable handlebars, handlebars that curved up to the
hands from under the back of the legs (supposed to allow a thrown
rider to fly through the air feet, rather than head, first) and lever
devices permitting the rider to sit over the back, rather than the front,
wheel. The "Star" bicycle, which mounted the small wheel in front
rather than behind, was the most successful solution: it was stable
enough to be ridden down the steps of the Capitol in Washington.

⊛ BIKE POLITICS ⊛

The late 1960s and early 1970s were the dog days of cycling in
Britain. Public policy had for many years made the car king and
the negative impact of auto-culture on city living was not yet widely
understood, with a typical view being that the city had to adapt to the
presence of the car rather than vice versa. Ernest Marples declared
in 1967 that he would not ride a bike in London because, "if you try
and go round Hyde Park Corner on a cycle you are signing your own
death warrant" – a disgraceful admission, given that only a few years
previously he had been Minister of Transport.

Small wonder that the number of miles cycled in Britain
plummeted by 80 per cent during the period. Happily, times have

changed; while in the late 1970s only 4,000 hardy souls dared to commute into central London by bike, in the 21st century many times that number do – and the city's public Cycle Hire Scheme took only a few months to record one million "Boris Bike" journeys within central London. Some attitudes are harder to shift, though: in early 2011, Eric Pickles MP (Conservative Secretary of State for Communities and Local Government) ridiculed cyclists for their "rubber knickers" and called for the government to end its "war on the motorist".

━━━━━━━━━━━━━━━

"I hope that cycling in London will become almost Chinese in its ubiquity."

Boris Johnson (Mayor of London)

⊛ CYCLE TO WORK ⊛

One British government initiative which has succeeded is the "Cycle to Work" scheme. This allows commuters to buy their bike through their employer and pay for it in monthly instalments. Not only does this spread the cost over a year, it also means that the bike is VAT-free. And, because it's paid for out of gross income before tax, the total saving is typically 50 per cent. In 2010, the Cycle to Work Alliance reported that the additional cycle commuters which the scheme had created had saved 133,442 tons of carbon emissions – the same as the annual emissions from a small town. Sixty-one per cent of them would not have started cycle commuting without the scheme; 98 per cent would recommend it to their colleagues.

⊛ ROAD TAX NONSENSE ⊛

Next time a conversational motorist tells you that they are paying for the road you're cycling on – and therefore that you are a second-class road user – you can confidently reply this is not the case. "Road Tax" does not exist: the link between vehicle taxation and expenditure on roads in the UK was abolished as long ago as 1937. The correct term for the tax that motorists pay is "Vehicle Excise Duty" and it has nothing to do with the money that government spends on the roads, which comes from the general taxation pool. Go to the splendid (ironically-named) website *ipayroadtax.com* to find out more...

⊛ BIG NUMBERS ⊛

The largest bicycle manufacturing countries in Europe are Italy and Germany, which each turn out around 2.5 million every year. Italy is a net exporter of bikes, Germany is a net importer. The giant is of course China, which makes tens of millions every year.

———————

In 2010, sales of bicycles in the UK broke the four million mark for the first time.

⊛ IN PRAISE OF BIKES ⊛

"When man invented the bicycle he reached the peak of his attainments. Here was a machine of precision and balance for the convenience of man. And (unlike subsequent inventions for man's convenience) the more he used it, the fitter his body became. Here, for once, was a product of man's brain that was entirely beneficial to those who used it, and of no harm or irritation to others. Progress should have stopped when man invented the bicycle."

Elizabeth West (author) in *Hovel in the Hills*

———————

"... the bicycle is the most efficient machine ever created: converting calories into gas, a bicycle gets the equivalent of 3,000 miles per gallon."

Bill Strickland (author) in *The Quotable Cyclist*

⊛ HAPPY PRESIDENTS ⊛

"I like riding a bicycle built for two – by myself."

Harry S. Truman (former US President)

———————

"Nothing compares to the simple pleasure of a bike ride."

John F. Kennedy (former US President)

◉ LONGFELLOW ◉

Turn, turn, my wheel! Turn round and round,
Without a pause, without a sound:
So spins the flying world away!

H.W. Longfellow (poet) in *Kéramos*, 1878

◉ ALBERT A. POPE ◉

The most influential figure in the early years of American cycling was Colonel Albert A Pope. In order to ensure dominance for his Columbia machines (first manufactured in 1878) he hired champions like Will Pitman, founded clubs, distributed books and magazines, and campaigned for – and on occasion financed – better roads. He also offered rewards for the return of stolen Columbias – but not other bikes – to their rightful owners.

"Man is the animal which rides."

Charles Pratt (lawyer and cycling advocate) in
***The American Bicycler,* 1879**

◉ OBREE'S OLD FAITHFUL ◉

Graeme Obree had one of the most distinguished careers in the history of British cycling, yet he never even turned professional. In the space of three years he revolutionized track cycling, winning the world 4,000m pursuit title twice and twice breaking the hour record: yet his career was dogged by depression and he often struggled to find form.

His free-thinking, unconventional yet effective approach was perfectly summed up by the bicycle he made himself, and on which he made many of his best rides. Named "Old Faithful", this unique machine was constructed from stems of old (unused) BMX tubing (found bundled in the toilet of a cycle shop), a centre beam of Reynolds tandem tubing (specially ordered), rear drop outs made from old padlocks, a crank made from scrap found on the side of a road and a bottom bracket made from the bearings of an old washing machine. It was this last component that generated the most comment – not to say ridicule – but it worked well and, crucially, was much narrower than conventional bottom brackets, allowing Obree to bring his legs closer together and achieve a more aerodynamic profile. The only component he didn't make himself were the state-of-the-art Specialized wheels – with tyres pumped to over 200psi, an enormous pressure.

***

"Old Faithful" is honoured in the name of one of Bitish cycling's most distinctive blogs, *the washing machine post* (*www.thewashingmachinepost.net*), which celebrates two-wheeled life on Islay, where it admits that "the roads are not in possession of a glass-like surface" but where it is true that "cycle theft [is] almost non-existent" and the annual Sportive glories in the name of the "Ride of the Falling Rain".

◉ MAKE IT YOURSELF ◉

Former pro racer Tom Simpson made his own saddles, combining plastic, leather and foam in a way that was startlingly innovative for the late-1950s and standard today.

***

"Today I am going to amuse the public by riding an 86-inch bicycle to Trumpington and back… It is great fun riding this leviathan: it creates such an extraordinary sensation among the old dons who happen to be passing."

The Honorable Ion Keith-Falconer (an early amateur champion) in an 1878 letter

◉ THE JERSEYS OF THE TOUR DE FRANCE ◉

Yellow   Leader in the General Classification (GC)   (1919–)
Worn by the rider with the lowest aggregate time in the whole race – effectively, the race's fastest rider. The colour was chosen to match the paper that L'Auto, the newspaper that launched the Tour, was printed on. Eddy Merckx spent longest in yellow – 96 days in total.

Polka Dot   King of the Mountains   (1933–)
Worn by the best climber, decided on a points system. Those over the top of the climbs first gain most points. The polka-dot jersey was introduced in 1975, though there was a mountain competition from 1933.

Green   Leader in the points (sprint) competition   (1953–)
Effectively worn by the best sprinter, decided on a points system. Riders reaching certain pre-marked intermediate lines first during a stage, as well as the first to the finish, earn most points. The first sponsor was a lawnmower manufacturer – hence the green.

White   Best Young Rider in the GC   (1975–)
Worn by the young rider with the lowest aggregate time. Riders must be under 26 on the first day of the year to qualify.

There are also two defunct jerseys:

Combination   Best rider across all categories   (1968–89)
Initially plain white, and from 1975 white, with red, green, yellow, red and polka-dot panels, the combination jersey never really captured the imagination and it was only awarded in 15 Tours. Eddy Merckx won it five times.

Red   Leader in the intermediate sprints competition   (1984–89)
Points from this old sprint competition now count toward the green jersey instead (see above).

◉ THE JERSEYS OF THE GIRO D'ITALIA ◉

The awarding of jerseys on the Tour of Italy follows the same principles as for the Tour de France (see previous entry).

Pink   Leader in the General Classification (GC)   (1931–)
La Gazetta dello Sport, the newspaper which organized the first Giro, is printed on pink paper – hence the pink.

| **Green** | Leader of the Mountains Classification | (1974–) |

Legendary Italian rider Gino Bartali won the green jersey seven times.

| **Mauve** | Leader of the points (sprint) classification | (1970–2009) |

| **Red** | Leader of the points (sprint) classification | (1967–69, 2010–) |

The first winner of the re-introduced red jersey was Australian Cadel Evans.

| **White** | Best Young Rider in the GC | (1976–94, 2007–) |

| **Black** | Last rider in the GC | (1946–51) |

The rider with the highest aggregate time – effectively the race's slowest rider.

❀ BLACK JERSEY BLUES ❀

The last rider to be issued with the Giro D'Italia's black jersey was Giovanni Pinarello. His sponsor, Bottecchia, paid off his contract in order to replace him on the team. With this money, Pinarello opened a bike shop in Treviso and went on to become one of Italy's most famous bike manufacturers.

❀ *CIMA COPPI* ❀

The highest point reached by the route of the Giro D'Italia on any given year is designated the *Cima Coppi* – the Coppi Summit – in honour of Fausto Coppi, five-time winner of the race, who died in 1960 of malaria at the age of only 40.

❀ DON'T BOTHER COMING ❀

Alfredo Binda won the Giro d'Italia in 1925, 1927, 1928, 1929 and 1933. He sat out the 1930 race having been paid 22,500 lire – more than the winner's prize money – not to compete. The organizers wanted someone else to win in order to maintain the public's interest.

⊕ THE JERSEYS OF THE VUELTA A ESPANA ⊕

The awarding of jerseys for the Tour of Spain follows the same principles as for the Tour de France (see pages 135–6) but the jerseys of the Vuelta have frequently changed.

Leader in the General Classification (GC)	Orange (1935–40), White (1941), Orange (1942–44), White with a horizontal red stripe (1945–50), Yellow (1955–76), Orange (1977), Yellow (1978–97), Gold (1998–2009), Red (2010–) *Alex Zülle of Swizerland has spent longest in the leader's jersey: 48 days.*
Points Classification	This jersey has changed many times over the years. A recurring theme is blue, with a pattern of yellow fish – as the shirt's sponsor is often the Spanish fishing industry.
King of the Mountains	Jersey colours also vary. Designs have included white spots on a red shirt, plain grey, brown coffee beans on a white shirt (when Café de Colombia sponsored the competition) and green. It is currently white with blue spots.

⊕ THE RAINBOW JERSEY OF THE WORLD CHAMPIONSHIP ⊕

The jersey is white, with horizontal stripes (from top to bottom: blue, red, black, yellow and green). The colours were chosen to match those of the Olympic rings (in an Olympic year, the Olympic competition doubles as the World Championships) and also reflect the colours in the flags of the major European cycling nations.

Cycling is unique among major sports in that the honours a rider wins while racing for their country must be sported year-round as they race as an individual or a member of a professional team in that discipline (failure to do so is punishable by a fine from the UCI). Another unique detail is that former world champions are entitled to sport piping in the rainbow pattern on the cuffs and collars of their jerseys for the rest of their careers.

The first World Championship event was the 10km track sprint, won by Arthur Zimmerman of the US in 1894. Since then, the number of disciplines and events has grown considerably, with a proliferation in recent years: over 50 separate riders (of both sexes) may now wear the rainbow jersey each year. These are the current professional events that can earn riders a world champions rainbow jersey.

Discipline	Event	Inaugural Year (Men)	Inaugural Year (Women)
Road	Road Race	1927	1958
	Time Trial	1994	1994
Track	Sprint	1895	1958
	Team Sprint	1995	2007
	Time Trial	1993	1995
	Kierin	1980	2002
	Individual Pursuit	1946	1958
	Team Pursuit	1993	2008
	Scratch Race	2002	2002
	Points Race	1980	1988
	Madison	1995	–
	Omnium	2007	2009
Cyclo-Cross		1950	2000
Mountain Bike	Marathon	2005	2005
	Cross-Country	1990	1990
	Downhill	1990	1990
	4-Cross	2002	2002
	Team Relay	1999	–
Trial	20" Wheel	1992	2001
	26" Wheel	1996	–
BMX		1996	1996

⊛ LA GRANDE BOUCLE ⊛

The women's edition of the Tour de France is formally known as *La Grande Boucle* because the organizers of the men's Tour (itself informally known as *La Grande Boucle*) objected to the name *Tour Cycliste Féminin*. The race, first run in 1984, has faced difficulties and now only lasts five or six days. Of late, the British have been the most successful nation, with Nicole Cooke winning the event twice and Emma Pooley once.

⊛ GIRO DONNE ⊛

The women's version of the Giro D'Italia is the *Giro D'Italia Femminile,* or *Giro Donne*. Made up of 10 stages around northern Italy, it has been run since 1988. Fabiana Luperini of Italy has won it six times.

⊛ BERYL BURTON RULES ⊛

It's a fair assumption that no other racer has ever enjoyed the same level of dominance in their field as the legendary Beryl Burton. She won the UCI World Championship Road Race twice, coming second once. On the track, she won the World Championship Pursuit title five times, coming second and third three times, too. (Between 1959 and 1968, she was in the rainbow jersey for six seasons: in his pomp, Eddy Merckx managed three.)

If Burton's international record was impressive, her consistency at home was nothing less than awesome. She won the Road Time Trials Council's "British Best All-Rounder" Competition for 25 consecutive years from 1959 to 1983. Her finest single achievement may have been setting a 12-hour time trial record that no man of the time could match; in doing so, she passed the male champion time-trialler Mike McNamara, reputedly handing him a Liquorice Allsort as she did so. She never turned professional: at one point she picked rhubarb as a day job.

⊛ HANS RENOLD'S CHAIN ⊛

The steel roller chain was invented by Hans Renold, a Swiss mechanic who settled in Manchester, in 1880. An elegant and successful design, it was a huge improvement on the pin chain which "safety" (early chain-driven) bicycles used and is still in use today. To properly lubricate the chain, it's necessary to get oil inside the cylinders (bushings) that your gears' teeth catch – you may find it's easiest to rest the bike on its left side to accomplish this. Wipe excess from the outside of the chain when you're done to stop it from attracting dirt.

Former track legend Graeme Obree contested, and won, many time trials using a single-speed bike – an unusual choice.

⊛ SIMPSON LEVER CHAIN ⊛

French artist Henri de Toulouse-Lautrec was a keen fan of the velodrome, although his physical disabilities prevented him from ever riding a bike. He did, however, produce a poster advertising the Simpson Lever Chain, a short-lived patent device erroneously thought to be more efficient than the standard model (French champion Hélène Dutrieu used a Simpson). It showed two five-man multicycles failing to catch up with a single rider on a Simpson-equipped bike.

⊛ MECHANICAL MARVEL ⊛

The chain drive is one of the most efficient transmissions known to engineering. A new, lubricated single-speed chain drive can be 98.5 per cent efficient, losing only 1.5 per cent of power to friction – so long as it has more than about 12 teeth on the rear sprocket. Well-maintained derailleur systems tend to be more efficient than hub gear systems, and are at their most efficient in low gear.

⊛ GEARING ⊛

Gearing is one of the most technically competitive areas of bike design. Pros are already adopting electric and electronic derailleurs, and computer-aided design tools have allowed sophisticated hub gears to compete with them. Sturmey-Archer – whose classic three-speed hub, patented in 1902, was near-ubiquitous on domestic bikes – now manufacture eight-speed hubs. Shimano have an 11-speed and German company Rohloff have a 14-speed. All are impressively durable and incredibly clever designs. Being resistant to mud and grime, and very low-maintenance, they are especially popular with mountain bikers and touring riders. They are, however, heavy, weighing in at nearly 2kg (4.5lb), so are avoided by racers.

---

*"I still feel that variable gears are only for people over 45.
Isn't it better to triumph by the strength of your muscles
than by the artifice of a derailleur? We are getting soft...
As for me, give me a fixed gear!"*

Henri Desgrange (founder of the Tour de France), 1902

⊛ RACING CONFIGURATIONS ⊛

Apart from the bunch or *peloton*, there are three configurations in which road racers can find themselves.

1. The Line (or Paceline)

Riders cycle directly behind each other in single file: the first in line holds the pace ("takes a pull") for as long as he or she can (this can be minutes or seconds), forcing their way through the air and creating a slipstream. The rider behind only has to expend about 75 per cent of the energy to maintain the same speed as the first in line: those behind him, even less. As soon as the leader is unable to hold this speed, they pull to one side and (without braking) allow the line to move past. They then rejoin the line at the end. As the other riders in turn reach the front, tire and return to the back of the line, the first one slowly moves forward until it is time to take a pull again – a circulation known as "through and off". This very efficient formation allows a continuous high pace to be maintained for comparatively little effort – as any rider is only working flat out for a short time. (In a line of four, for instance, a minute's pulling is rewarded with three minutes' recovery time.)

In a team time-trial, riders from the same team line up behind each other. It is a disaster, though, if the lead rider lets the pace of the whole line drop, so team-mates will encourage him or her to drop back and let fresh legs take over. It is common for the rules of such events to permit one or more of the team to drop off altogether, leaving only the very strongest riders in line to push the team to the finish. On a stage race, the *domestiques* may use the line formation to drag their leader through the early parts of a stage, allowing him to conserve his energy for later climbs or sprints.

If a line forms of competing riders, the dynamic is more complicated. A rider may deliberately take a short pull at the front, then drop off and, letting the competition do the hard work, be fresh for a later attack. This unscrupulous behaviour means that such lines exist in a state of continuous watchfulness and may not last long before either disintegrating altogether, or re-forming into the less-efficient – but impossible to cheat – ball formation.

2. The Ball Formation

The ball is an ingenious evolution of the line formation. The basic principle – riders constantly exchanging places to share the effort of overcoming wind resistance – is the same. Despite its name, a ball resembles two lines riding in parallel to one another – and to a roadside observer, appearing to move at the same pace. In fact, one line accelerates and the other (slightly) decelerates next to it.

As riders come to the front of the accelerating line they immediately move over to the front of the slower line and drop backward, recovering slightly from their exertions (and benefiting from an additional reduction in wind resistance caused by riding side-by-side). As they reach the rear of this file, they move back across to the accelerating side and the cycle begins again.

It's harder work than being in a single-file line, but the ball can be faster and the constant rotation that gives the formation its name means that shirking is impossible: for this reason it is often adopted by a group of cyclists from different teams, with a shared interest in making fast progress together tempered by a healthy dose of mutual suspicion.

3. The Echelon

An echelon forms when the peloton hits a strong cross-wind and is one of the most unpredictable of the cycling formations. It resembles a line strung out diagonally across the road, with the leader to the windward side and those behind capturing the slipstream as it is blown laterally across the road by the wind.

The echelon may operate in the same way as a line, but it is harder to organize and the efficiency gains are lower as the slipstream is disrupted by the crosswind.

Going into echelon often disrupts the field – a canny rider in the bunch may anticipate the wind, and quickly secure a good position in the echelon. A rider caught by surprise may find themselves far behind the leaders as the bunch is re-shaped into a long series of echelons – and the strong crosswind will make advancing solo through the field hard work.

◉ WIND RESISTANCE & DRAFTING ◉

Wind resistance does not increase proportionately in relation to your speed, but exponentially. This chart shows how its strength increases between a slow 10mph (16km/h) and a brisk 25mph (40km/h). The exact figure will vary according to your aerodynamic profile and other factors like air pressure and temperature: for this reason the vertical axis does not have numbers.

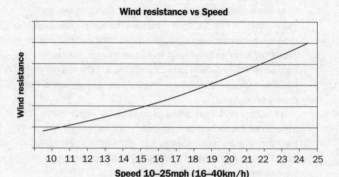

Wind resistance vs Speed

Wind resistance

10 11 12 13 14 15 16 17 18 19 20 21 22 23 24 25

Speed 10–25mph (16–40km/h)

Raising your pace from 10mph (16km/h) to 14mph (23km/h) almost doubles wind resistance. Increasing your speed to 20mph (32km/h) quadruples the wind resistance – and significantly increases the work you need to put into overcoming it.

◉ RELATIVE ENERGY CONSUMPTION ◉

It requires twice as much energy to ride at 32km/h (20mph) on an upright, roadster bicycle than a lightweight, aerodynamic racing machine. A recumbent bicycle requires even less energy – about half what the racing bike demands.

◉ DRAFTING: WIN–WIN ◉

Drafting not only helps a cyclist follow a leader, but gives the leader a boost as well. A solo cyclist leaves turbulent eddies and vortices in the air behind, which slightly increase drag. A slipstreaming rider following close behind stops this turbulence from forming by filling the space, giving the leader a slight but measurable boost.

⊛ A STEP TOO FAR... ⊛

British Olympian Ed Clancy (who was part of the gold-medal winning Team Pursuit team at the Beijing 2008 Olympics) has broad shoulders which make him slightly less aerodynamically efficient than he might be. Before the Olympics, he and team coach Dave Brailsford gave serious thought to deliberately breaking his collarbones so that they could be surgically re-set in a more efficient alignment. "But then, thankfully," relates Brailsford, "someone said, 'what on earth are you doing?' and this madness was stopped."

⊛ ETHICS AND THE WHEELSUCKER ⊛

Most of the time, it is morally incumbent on all the members of a line to take a pull in turn. Failure to do so – gaining from others' hard work without returning the favour – is regarded as a serious offence against the racers' informal code of honour. There are, of course, exceptions. A team leader, or top sprinter, may be "pulled" for many miles by his *domestiques* – on the understanding, of course, that when the time comes, he will return the favour by spending the energy thereby saved on the crucial climb, or in the sprint for the line.

A rider who has crashed may likewise be helped back to the group by a colleague in order to help him recover. At an amateur level some will let the "wheelsucker" remain on the back of the line if they are confident that he will not steal past them at the finish and take their glory. If they do so, of course, they will be the subject of some opprobrium...

"The wheelsucker is full-time vermin, a rat in perpetuity. The rat is invisible, hidden, non-existent until 100m from the finish, when he suddenly heaves himself into action, his one and only effort, under – if not up – the noses of those who have built up and led the race over many, many kilometres. Wherever you went, the wheelsucker was regarded as excrement. He still is, I'm told."

Jean Bobet (author and former pro cyclist) in
Tomorrow We Ride

✪ WHEELSUCKER FINGER POINTING ✪

Australian pro Cadel Evans has had to defend himself from
repeated allegations of wheelsucking on his way to a string
of top 10 Tour placings. He claims that he simply rides to his
strengths. "Why should I attack guys who are better climbers
than me – what's the point?" he asks. But others, including rival
Alexandre Vinokourov, take a different view. In the Dutch media,
Evans has even been referred to as *Meister Aanklamper* –
Master Wheelsucker.

*"I keep taking my pull, then look back. Reilhan doesn't take
his. I drop back, and we ride on beside each other in
amazement and silence. This is really going too far…"*

Tim Krabbé (author) in *The Rider*

✪ PEDALLING EFFICIENCY ✪

Scientists have plotted the energy efficiency of different forms of
human movement, from walking and swimming up to diesel train
and car. The bike is by far the most efficient – at 15km/h (9mph)
it's three times more efficient than running and well over 10 times
more efficient than driving in a car at 50km/h (30mph).

Improving your pedalling action is an excellent way to make the
journey faster, smoother and better for you. The first step is to
use cleated shoes and clip-on pedals, which allow you to put
some power into the upstroke. Try to avoid up-down-up-down
pedalling, instead aiming for a smooth circular action. *Bicycling*
magazine recommends you pull through at the bottom as if trying
to scrape something off the sole of your shoe, and over at the
top as if trying to bump your knee against the handlebar.

One technique traditionally used by pros is to concentrate for a
minute at a time on a smooth movement through one particular
part of the stroke: the rest of your action will benefit. Finally,
riders of fixed-gear bikes swear that their machines, which do
not allow the rider to stop pedalling and freewheel, inculcate the
best action of all.

⊛ GO BRAND-FREE ⊛

Most new bikes sold these days arrive with large decals advertising the manufacturer's brand. If you happen to find these unattractive, or an unnecessary magnet to thieves, or you simply don't want to ride around on a lurid bike advert, you may want to remove them.

Assuming they've not been varnished over along with the bike's paint job (in which case, it's probably best not to bother), the easiest way to do this is with a hairdryer. Simply aim it at one end of the decal, on a high setting, and wait for the adhesive to melt and the logo to loosen. Lift it off, and continue heating and peeling along its length. Any residue of adhesive should come off if you polish it with a little WD-40 or similar lubricant. Et voilà! Your bike's beautiful lines are now free of unsightly commercial clutter.

⊛ CYCLOSPORTIVES ⊛

The first Cycloportive (or simply Sportive) event was the inaugural edition of the French event *La Marmotte* in 1982: since the late 1990s, their popularity has rapidly grown and there are now over 600 sportive events held worldwide each year. Aimed at the keen amateur, but with many of the amenities of pro racing (closed roads, feed stations, electronic timing and so on), they all offer long routes, usually 100–200km (62–124 miles) and an opportunity to ride alongside hundreds or thousands of other enthusiasts. Most are less arduous than *La Marmotte,* which features over 5,000 vertical metres (16,400ft) in climbs and finishes at the top of the infamous Alpe d'Huez, used in the Tour de France.

⊛ SPORTIVE SABOTAGE ⊛

The British cyclosportive scene is developing all the time, with new races entering the calendar every year. At present, only one (L'Etape Caledonia in Perthshire) is run on traffic-free roads: in 2009, the event was sabotaged when thousands of carpet tacks were scattered on the roads in protest at the road closure, causing hundreds of riders to puncture. A local councillor was arrested in connection with the attack three days later, but charges were subsequently dropped. The event benefited from the resulting publicity and the 2010 and 2011 events were both sell-outs.

⊛ TRIATHLONS ⊛

The term "triathlon" was not coined until 1974, when a swim/ cycle/run event was organized by the San Diego Track club in the USA. (Much earlier, there had been similar races in France, which combined cycling with running and either swimming or canoeing.) Since then, the triathlon has become one of the most popular cycling disciplines despite its considerable physical challenges. Modern triathlon bikes may have a steep seat-tube angle in order to demand less from the muscles that the competitor will need for their run; often they also have "tri-bars", which extend the rider's arms and torso into a more aerodynamically efficient position (triathletes spend less time riding in a bunch, so the sacrifice of manoeuvrability is worth it).

⊛ AUDAX EVENTS ⊛

If you want a more arduous event than a sportive, but don't feel up to the running and swimming of the triathlon, then an "audax" event might be for you. A product of the Heroic era of the late 1890s and early 1900s, the format originated in France and was initially regulated by the magazine *L'Auto* and its proprietor Henri Desgrange (the hour record-holder who also established the Tour de France). Simply put, the event involved riding a very long way within a fixed time period: the most famous event is the Paris–Brest–Paris run, a 1,200km (746-mile) race which was only run once a decade and discontinued after seven events in 1951. (The last winner was the sportsmanlike Maurice Diot, who completed the race in a phenomenal 38hr 55min; he beat Edouard Muller in sprint finish, having stopped and waited 22km (14 miles) from the finish as Muller repaired a puncture.) After an administrative schism typical of cycle sport, the modern, ostensibly less competitive, event evolved.

In order to enter Paris–Brest–Paris, a rider must have a certificate demonstrating that they have completed a 600km 373-mile) ride in under 24 hours. So that British riders had a chance to qualify, the first British audax event, Windsor–Chester– Windsor, was launched in 1976, and the calendar is now full of events ranging in length from 100–1,400km (62–870 miles), the longest distance representing the London–Edinburgh– London ride.

The jewel in the crown of European audax rides is probably Calais–Brindisi, which takes in 2,600km (1,615 miles) of riding in 13 days. The ride starts in the French Channel port, and finishes in Italy, facing Albania across the Adriatic. In case you were wondering, *audax* is originally a Latin word, and may be translated as brave, bold – or foolhardy.

◉ RACE ACROSS AMERICA ◉

The leading American audax event is the Race Across America or RAAM. 4,800km (3,000 miles) long, run from West to East. This annual event was won five times by the late Jure Robi, a Slovenian athlete who was killed in a crash with a car while out on a training run in his homeland. Taking in 12 states between San Diego, California and Annapolis, Maryland, it typically takes about eight days to complete and the winner may sleep for only eight hours in that time: only the early Madison events have made similar demand, and they were declared illegal a century ago.

◉ TAIL-ENDERS ◉

The slowest rider in the Tour de France is sometimes called the *lanterne rouge* or red lantern and traditionally carried a small red light beneath his saddle. Such was public sympathy for this humiliation that he could command higher fees in the round-the-houses races that followed the Tour. In two Tours (1939 and 1948), the organizers tried to encourage a more competitive spirit by disqualifying the last rider to finish each day's stage.

A stage race's *commissaires* will disqualify riders who do not finish within a certain period after the leader. This threat is designed to make sure that everyone puts in an effort on all stages and often results in a small group (the *gruppetto*) of stragglers cutting it fine just ahead of the "broom wagon" (the bus which brings up the rear, sweeps up the laggards and informally marks the slowest pace before disqualification). There can be exceptions, however. If a rider had to make ground up after an accident, if the stage was run particularly fast, if the rider made especially heroic efforts to catch up, or if they were hampered by traffic, then the *commissaires* may be lenient and let a slow rider survive to ride another day.

◉ SWEPT UP BY THE BROOM WAGON ◉

The French for broom wagon, the vehicle that picks up stragglers and the back of a road race, is *voiture balai*. For many years the van performing this function at all kinds of races was the distinctive Citroën H, instantly recognizable by its corrugated side panels and huge porcine radiator grille, which earned it the nickname *nez de cochon* (pig nose). The *voiture balai* does indeed carry a broom – except if, as has happened, it is sponsored that year by a maker of vacuum cleaners.

An alternative English term is "Sag Wagon", derived from the abbreviation of "Supplies and Gear", which the wagon may also carry in the absence of team cars.

The wonderful animated cycling movie *Belleville Rendez-Vous* features a *voiture balai* bringing up the rear of the Tour.

◉ KEEP ON MOVING ◉

"Ever bike? Now that's something that makes life worth living! I take exercise every afternoon that way. Oh, to just grip your handlebars and lay down to it, and go ripping and tearing through streets and road, over railroad tracks and bridges, threading crowds, avoiding collisions, at 20 miles or more an hour, and wondering all the time when you're going to smash up. Well, now, that's something! And then go home again after three hours of it... and then to think that tomorrow I can do it all over again!"

Jack London (author) in a letter to a friend

"When do we ever feel so free, so full of joie de vivre, as when we're on a bike? When do we ever feel so much a part of the landscape, such oneness with earth and sky?"

Greg Bassham (professor of philosophy and author)

◉ BIKE FOR LIFE ◉

"I never want to abandon my bike. I see my grandfather, now in his seventies and riding around everywhere. To me that is beautiful. And the bike must always remain a part of my life."

Stephen Roche (former pro cyclist)

"When the spirits are low, when the day appears dark, when work becomes monotonous, when hope hardly seems worth having, just mount a bicycle and go out for a spin down the road, without thought on anything but the ride you are taking."

Sir Arthur Conan Doyle (author)

Cycling does it all – you have the complete satisfaction of arriving because your mind has chosen the path and steered you over it; your eyes have seen it; your muscles have felt it; your breathing, circulatory and digestive systems have all done their natural functions better than ever, and every part of your being knows you have traveled and arrived.

John Forester (author) in *Effective Cycling*

◉ THE FUTURE'S BRIGHT ◉

"When I see an adult on a bicycle, I do not despair for the future of the human race."

H.G. Wells (author)

"We think it an invention which will not have an ephemeral popularity, but which will ... revolutionise travel for all time."

J.T. Goddard (author) in *The Velocipede*, 1869

◉ LANCE ARMSTRONG: "ONE BIG LIE" ◉

Sad to relate, the sensational career of Lance Armstrong is undoubtedly the biggest story that cycling has known. There is a huge literature devoted to the subject: spare yourself many depressing reads, and acquaint yourself with the key facts of his fraud, with this timeline.

1971   Lance Gunderson is born in Plano, Texas, on September 18th. He is named after Lance Rentzel, Dallas Cowboys running back.

1974   He is adopted by his stepfather, Terry Armstrong.

1984   At thirteen, he wins his first junior triathlon.

1987   At sixteen, becomes a professional triathlete, and in 1989 and 1990 he is US national sprint-course triathlon champion.

1992   He turns pro with Motorola.

1993   In July, has his first stage win at the Tour de France, but retires after twelve stages. Meets journalist David Walsh for the first time: Walsh, almost infatuated, devotes a glowing chapter in his book Inside the Tour de France to the young rider. In August, wins the UCI World Road Championship road race, beating Miguel Indurain into second place.

1994   Armstrong struggles, with second place in Liège—Bastogne—Liège his best result. Some experts suggest that this was the year in which EPO use became widespread in the peloton, driving up speeds and putting Armstrong at a disadvantage.

1995   A better year, with a Tour de France stage win. Teammate George Hincapie will later recall that Armstrong first suggested using EPO after they were "crushed" in Milan—San Remo that March. At the end of the year Armstrong is introduced (by Eddy Merckx) to the Italian doctor Michele Ferrari.

1996   Wins La Flèche Wallone, but only completes five stages of the Tour de France. Signs for Cofidis in August. On October 2nd, Armstrong is diagnosed with advanced testicular cancer; an operation the following day is followed by two months of chemotherapy and a further operation to remove secondary tumours in his brain. On October 23rd, team-mate Frankie Andreu, his wife, and several others witness a conversation with his doctors during which Armstrong admits to using "EPO, testosterone, growth hormone, cortisone and steroids".

1997 Is dropped by Cofidis in February, and offered a contract (at one tenth of the value) by US Postal. Visits the Tour as a spectator: starts planning his comeback, as he continues his recovery. His illness, and his treatment, have reduced his weight significantly, giving him a lighter physique more suited to the dominant climbs that will underpin his success.

1998 Wins the Tour of Luxembourg and comes fourth in the Vuelta a Espana. This year's Tour de France sees the Festina scandal: later analysis of blood samples taken from riders confirms that the top three finishers (Marco Pantani, Jan Ullrich, Bobby Julich) and green jersey winner Eric Zabel were all using EPO. At least 50 riders are known to have doped in the race. Armstrong does not compete.

1999 Johan Bruyneel takes over as director of US Postal: later testimony from team-mate Tyler Hamilton confirms that Armstrong and other riders are using EPO "every third or fourth day, until the third week of the Tour" (when his lead was large enough to be unassailable). A urine test reveals steroid use, but a team doctor issues a back-dated prescription claiming that Armstrong needs corticosteroid for saddle sores. On Stage 10, Armstrong confronts Christophe Bassons, an attack which results in Bassons leaving the Tour—and the first doubts in David Walsh's mind that Armstrong might not be clean. Lance wins the Tour: "This afternoon I will be keeping my arms by my side," Walsh writes after the finish, "because I'm not sure this is something we should be applauding."

2000 On May 22nd, *It's Not About The Bike* is published. In it, Armstrong writes: 'Doping is an unfortunate fact of life in cycling, or any other endurance sport for that matter. Inevitably, some teams and riders feel it's like nuclear weapons—that they have to to do it to stay competitive within the peloton. I never felt that way... I had extremely mixed feelings about the 1998 Tour: I sympathized with the riders, some of whom I knew well, but I also felt the Tour would be a more fair event from then on.' On 23rd July, Armstrong crosses the line in Paris wearing the yellow jersey: the second of his Tour wins.

2001 Armstrong again wins the Tour de France. His performance includes a dominant ride up the Alpe d'Huez: standing out of the saddle for minutes on end, dropping the competition with arrogant ease, and causing commentators to remark on his 'poker face'. From examining hotel registers, David Walsh discovers that Armstrong has been visiting Dr Michele Ferrari in secret.

2002 In February, the Italian rider Filippo Simeoni, publicly testifies that he had been prescribed EPO by Dr Michele Ferrari five years earlier. In May, Armstrong secretly donates $25,000 to the UCI, who spend the money on drug testing in junior races. The Tour organisers create a course that is 600Km shorter than the 1998 edition in order to make doping less attractive to the riders. Armstrong takes the yellow jersey.

2003 In a June interview with French newspaper *Le Monde*, Armstrong calls Simeoni a liar for linking Ferrari to EPO abuse. His second volume of memoirs, *Every Second Counts* is published on October 7th. In it he writes: 'There was no mystery and no miracle drug that helped me win the Tour de France in 1999': In the same year, David Walsh and Pierre Ballaster interview Emma O'Reilly, who had been Armstrong's soigneur in 1999, and tells them a very different story. In the midst of this growing controversy, Lance again wins the Tour.

2004 Walsh and Ballaster's book, *L.A. Confidentiel : Les secrets de Lance Armstrong* is published in French: while it does not directly accuse Armstrong of doping, it sets out strong circumstantial evidence, including testimony from Emma O'Reilly that she helped Armstrong cover up doping. 'We don't actually prove anything," says Walsh. "We just set out the facts and let the reader decide for himself who's telling the truth." Armstrong sues The Sunday Times, Walsh's employers, in the UK courts, a case which continues for two years. Back on the road, there's an unsporting episode in which Armstrong threatens to neutralise a breakaway which Simeoni was part of. He is intimidated into dropping off: the peloton rallies behind their patron, subjecting Simeoni to a volley of saliva. Two days later, Simeoni takes his revenge, forcing the pace on the final stage—traditionally, taken at a slow speed to allow the yellow jersey to soak up the applause of the crowds. Once again, Lance wins the Tour.

2005 143 urine tests and 21 blood tests are conducted over the course of this year's Tour: none return positive results, although subsequently all three of the podium finishers will serve bans for doping (Jan Ullrich and Ivan Basso are the other two). Armstrong's average pace over the course of the Tour is 41.7 Km/h (26Mph), the highest recorded in the event's history. He records the last of his victories on July 24th and announces his retirement the same day, making a speech attacking "the people who don't believe in cycling, the cynics, the sceptics". He continues: "You need to believe in these riders. I'm sorry you can't dream big and I'm sorry you don't believe in miracles". In August, L'Equipe devotes four pages to allegations that fresh tests of 1999 urine samples have revealed evidence of EPO doping: Armstrong claims to be victim of a 'witch hunt'. Secretly, he donates $100,000 to the UCI, who use the money to buy a Sysmex blood testing machine.

2006 Armstrong's libel case against *The Sunday Times* finishes: he is awarded £300,000 in damages. On July 28, he calls in to The David Letterman Show to express his support for former team-mate Floyd Landis, who is facing a ban following a positive test for synthetic testosterone.

2008 On September 9, Armstrong announces his return to cycling and his intention of competing in the 2009 Tour.

2009 Riding for the Astana team, Armstrong places third in the Tour: his team-mate, Fabian Cancellara, wins. Before the start of the Tour of California, Armstrong confronts journalist—and friend of David Walsh—Paul Kimmage, over the latter's allegations of doping. His aggressive denial is viewed millions of times on Youtube: the rest of the journalists present seem to be on Armstrong's side.

2010 On May 20, former team-mate—and already-convicted doper—Floyd Landis releases emails containing his own confession of doping, and accusing Armstrong of using EPO and blood transfusions in 2002 and 2003. US federal prosecutors start a criminal investigation; initially they focus on Landis, but then shift their aim towards Armstrong.

2011 On February 16, Armstrong announces his retirement for the second time.

2012 On February 2, the US federal investigation is dropped, and no charges are brought: in June, the United States Anti-Doping Agency (USADA) accuses him of doping, and the edifice of his repeated angry denials finally starts to crumble. In July, USADA bans Michele Ferrari; on August 27, after a brief legal tussle, Armstrong drops his formal defence against USADA's charges, forfeiting all the titles that he had won, and earning himself a life ban. He maintains, though, his innocence, and speaks of a "witch hunt" and USADA's "outlandish and heinous claims". On September 5, former team-mate Tyler Hamilton publishes his memoir: *The Secret Race: Inside the Hidden World of the Tour de France: Doping, Cover-ups, and Winning at All Costs*. It details Armstrong's doping practices during their four years riding together. The UCI, which over the years has consistently failed to pursue Armstrong's doping, requests an explanation of USADA's charges. When published in October, the "reasoned decision" runs to over 1,200 pages, detailing failed drug tests, secret payments to Ferrari, witness intimidation, fraudulent misrepresentation, and at least sixteen years of lies. Two weeks later, the UCI strips Armstrong of all his post 1998 results. Pat McQuaid, President of the UCI—which had accepted Armstrong's money in 2002 and 2005, and consistently ignored the mounting evidence of his guilt in the years after 1999—says that Armstrong "deserves to be forgotten".

2013 On January 13, in a TV interview with Oprah Winfrey, Armstrong finally admits to doping during all of his Tour wins, and admits that his story was "one big lie".

⊛ SHIMANO-GO-GO ⊛

Despite a commercial dominance of the component market dating back to the 1980s, Shimano only achieved its first Tour de France win in 2007.

━━━━━━━━━━━

Shimano don't only manufacture cycling componentry; the company diversified into angling equipment as long ago as 1970, and now also offers golf clubs, snowboards, and rowing equipment.

Campagnolo's efforts at diversifying its product range, on the other hand, have extended exactly as far as one corkscrew. The "BIG", as the foot-long beast is appropriately named, boasts precision engineering, distinctive design, and an eye-watering price tag of £160.

⊛ HATRED ⊛

"Well, it's not me. It's not me at all. It's hard work, really hard work, and it's incredibly draining. I hate it, I really hate it."

Victoria Pendleton (former World Champion, two-time Olympic gold medal winner)

"Everyone was complaining about jetlag. Mark [Cavendish] was pissed off, too, but he went to the Tour of Ireland and won three stages. It helped that Mark was pissed off. For racing, I'd rather he was pissed off. Then he wins. When cyclists get happy, it's not good."

Brian Holm, HTC team Manager

⊛ BEATING THE BOYS ⊛

Beryl Burton was not the last British woman to take on the men and win: in 2006, Shanaze Reade raced against them all year, becoming the British National BMX no.1 in the category of 19 and over elite men. She was 17 at the time, and had bought her first BMX bike for £1.

⊛ EBIKE FACTS ⊛

Graeme Obree famously built and rode a bike with the bearings of a washing machine where the bottom bracket usually sits. These days, washing machine manufacturer Bosch is also one of the biggest manufacturers of eBike motors and components.

The first eBikes appeared in the 1890s—early pioneers included the magnificently named Ogden Bolton Jr. and Hosea W. Libby—but it was not till the late 1990s that advances in battery technology made them affordable and practicable.

The largest market for eBikes is China, where over 150 million are in use, but they remain illegal in Hong Kong.

A 2012 city ordnance made eBikes illegal in New York, but they remain widely used by Manhattan's food delivery men—notoriously, a group with a 'relaxed' view of the law as it relates to cycling.

When is an eBike not a bike? Fortunately, an EU standard makes it relatively easy to define what is an eBike and what isn't. If the power output is 250W or less, power only engages when the rider turns the pedals, and the maximum speed is no more than 25 KpH, it counts as a bike: so you can ride on a cycle path, and without registering it as a motor vehicle. Similar standards apply in Australia. In the US, it's more complicated, with a baffling variety of rules enacted by individual states. In Alabama and Michigan, for instance, you must wear a motorcycle helmet to be legal, and about half the states require you to have a driver's licence. Small wonder that the US market for eBikes is tiny.

Over a 10-mile time trial, Bradley Wiggins claims an average power output of around 476 Watts – twice as powerful as a typical eBike. In the final thirty seconds of a sprint finish, though, a top rider may generate 1,500 Watts or more.

Perhaps unsurprisingly, the 1980s boom in BMX riding resulted in a parallel boom in BMX-riding injuries. A study conducted by C.M. Illingworth of Sheffield Children's Hospital analysed differences in hospital admissions between BMX and 'ordinary' bike riders: the latter group were nearly twice as likely to have sustained injuries above the neck, while BMX riders were more than twice as likely to have broken a limb. Both suffered badly from lacerations—'road rash', in cycling parlance.

⊛ WHERE DO 'MAMILS' SHOP ⊛

The term "Mamil" was coined in 2010 by one Michael Oliver, in a report for the marketing agency Mintel. It stands for "Middle-Aged Man in Lycra": according to Mintel's report, Mamils own expensive bikes, are often high earners, and their favourite supermarket is Waitrose.

⊛ ROCK MAMIL? ⊛

History does not record whether U2's Bono was wearing lycra, or indeed a helmet, when he fell from his bike in Central park in November 16th 2014, but we do know that he suffered a variety of nasty injuries in the event: doctors repaired a facial fracture to the orbit of his left eye, three fractures to the left scapula, six to the left elbow and one to his left little finger. The elbow repair alone required three metal plates and no fewer than 18 screws. Ow.

⊛ WET-WEATHER WARNING ⊛

In wet weather, conventional rim brakes require a stopping distance three to four times longer than they do under dry conditions. Maximize your brake efficiency in the wet by applying them gently from time to time to sweep water from the rims. Choose long and soft brake blocks: efficiency varies from manufacturer to manufacturer by a surprising amount, so don't be afraid to experiment.

⊛ EPIC RIDE ⊛

According to Guinness World Records, the record for the longest journey by bicycle in a single country is held by Prasad Erande, whose five-month trip around India saw him roll no fewer than 14576 km (9057.1 miles) at a rate of just over 58 miles per day.

⊛ SUB ZERO HERO ⊛

Perhaps the bravest (or foolhardiest) of all cycling record attempts is that made by Eric Larsen, who in 2012 attempted to ride across Antarctica to the South Pole. Riding a Surly Monlander 'Fat Bike' with oversized tyres and 40 kilos of equipment, Larsen was sadly forced to turn back when only a quarter of the way into his 800 mile odyssey. 'Surface snow conditions' were to blame for the attempt's failure, but Larsen's ride remains the longest on the Antarctic continent.

⊛ RICKSHAW HISTORY ⊛

The first cycle rickshaw was invented in the 1880s, but it was not until 1929 that they found regular use—in Singapore. Today they are widespread in European cities, although mainly used for sight-seeing rather than transport.

⊛ BE SAFE, BE SEEN ⊛

Recent advances in LED and battery technology have seen bicycle lamps improve beyond all recognition. Many models now emit up to 300 lumens, roughly equivalent to the brightness of a conventional 40W bulb.

⊛ WHAT IS THE HEMATOCRIT? ⊛

For about a decade – between EPO's emergence in the early 1990s and the development of more sophisticated testing in 2004 – it was impossible to detect EPO in the bloodstream or urine of a tested rider. Unlike the 'traditional' drugs of cycling's early years, EPO worked by stimulating the user's body to create more of an entirely natural performance enhancer: red blood cells. The more red cells you have in your blood, the more oxygen is transported to your muscles, and the better they will work. In a healthy, undoped, person, red blood cells account for less than half of the volume of the blood: this proportion, as a percentage, is known as the 'hematocrit' – unfortunately, a term that fans of pro cycling have become far too familiar with over recent years. In a healthy, undoped, person, red blood cells account for less than half of the volume of the blood, giving a hematocrit value of 50% or less. When EPO is involved, however, this figure rises: Marco Pantani's 1994 and 1995 values fluctuated between a presumably natural 45%, in March each year, and anything up to 60% during the grand tours. Bjarne Riis, the winner of 1996's Tour, was himself known as 'Mr 60 per cent' in the pro peloton. The sad implication is that these riders won famous victories with their bloodstreams carrying a third more haemoglobin than they naturally would

There is a significant downside to this rich blood, though: being this heavily loaded with red blood corpuscles makes it thicker, and this in turn can lead to heart failure. The 1990s saw a tragic spate of sudden, otherwise inexplicable, deaths in cycling: so often did heart attacks happen in the middle of the night, that some EPO users took to hooking themselves up to circulation monitors at bedtime. Woken by the machine's alarm if their pulse dropped too low, they would immediately mount a static bike in the bedroom and pedal until the blood was circulating again properly.

••••••••••••••••••••••

"The sudden death of a rat belonging to the Ex+EPO group, due to a cardiac episode, together with the increased CV risk profile, strongly suggest a high life risk associated to the continuous rhEPO doping."

Erythropoietin Doping as a Cause of Sudden Death in Athletes— an Experimental Study
Various authors, Coimbra University Press, 2010

••••••••••••••••••••••

Jean-Michel Rouet: Speaking of EPO, do your riders use it?

Dr Michele Ferrari: I don't prescribe this stuff. But one can buy EPO in Switzerland for example without a prescription, and if a rider does, that doesn't scandalize me. EPO doesn't fundamentally change the performance of a racer.

J-MR: In any case, (EPO) is dangerous! Ten Dutch riders have died in the last few years.

Dr MF: EPO is not dangerous, it's the abuse that is. It's also dangerous to drink 10 liters of orange juice.

Michele Ferrari, speaking in April 1994, after riders from the Gewiss team—for which he was doctor—took the top three places in la Fleche Wallone.

⊛ NOSE-BREATHING WONDERS ⊛

By making the blood a better carrier of oxygen, EPO reduces the strain on the other parts of the respiratory process – notably, the lungs and breathing. This gave rise to one of the most widely-remarked phenomena of the EPO era: the sight of a rider blazing uphill at a furious rate, dropping rivals in his wake, yet breathing smoothly with his mouth closed.

⊛ KNOW YOUR DOPER ⊛

"When I saw riders with fat arses climbing cols like aeroplanes, I understood what was happening",

Colombian rider, Luis Herrera.

⸱⸱⸱⸱⸱⸱⸱⸱⸱⸱⸱⸱⸱⸱⸱⸱⸱⸱⸱⸱⸱

"In contrast to my tour win the previous year, all I felt was relief – unadulterated pure relief. I'd fulfilled my professional obligations – I couldn't have imagined doping and not winning. But it was all business now. It didn't feel like sport any more. Winning this way had never been part of my dream."

David Millar, on winning his first stage as a doper.

⸱⸱⸱⸱⸱⸱⸱⸱⸱⸱⸱⸱⸱⸱⸱⸱⸱⸱⸱⸱⸱

"Of course, the Derny needs a good driver, preferably an ex-cyclist who knows you very well so they can read your suffering from a glimpse of your poise on the bike and the look in your eye. If they know you well enough, they can keep you on the edge of collapse and, in doing so, make you race-ready."

David Millar

☀ TRIVIA ☀

Greg LeMond's 1986 Tour de France win was the first to be achieved on a carbon-framed bike.

☀ ... AND MORE PAIN ☀

"The ability to reach oxygen debt late, to delay the onset of pain as lactic acid builds up in muscles because of deprivation of oxygen in the blood, helps separate champions from their fellow riders. Racers treasure the ability to suffer..."

Samuel Abt (cycling journalist) in *In High Gear*

"Cycling is unique. No other sport lets you go like that – where there's only the bike left to hold you up. If you ran as hard, you'd fall over. Your legs wouldn't support you."

Steve Johnson (cycling coach and administrator)

☀ 2013 TOUR ☀

"I went back last year for the 100th tour as a guest. Anyone who ever finished the Tour was put in a special stand by the Champs-Elysees and made a big deal of. They photographed us, told us we were giants of the road. It was f***ing great."

Paul Kimmage

✿ TOP FORM ✿

"Perfect 'form' is judged on everything from the pedalling action, the position on the bike, the attire that's worn and the style with which it is worn, to the way one carries oneself. The list goes on, but once you know how form is defined, you can judge it with a mere glance at a passing cyclist."

David Millar

✿ FIVE SIGNS OF GOOD 'FORM' ✿

1. Your hips and upper body don't move from side to side. A common cause of saddle sores is a too-high saddle forcing your backside to track over the saddle, rubbing each time. Drop your saddle slightly if you feel this happening. When you're on the saddle, your upper body shouldn't move much.
2. Elbows should be tucked in behind the forearm, and not project outwards.
3. Pedalling action should be smooth and even: concentrate particularly on the upward part of the rotation
4. Your legs should move up and down, but not in and out: keep the knees moving vertically, but not horizontally
5. When standing for extra power, tilt the bike – but not your body – very slightly from side to side to maximise pedalling efficiency. Even if you're standing, make sure that your legs, not your upper body, are doing the work.

✿ THE MAGIC OF LATEX ✿

Bored of punctures? Try one of the many liquid latex tyre sealants on the market today. Simply squirt half a bottle into the valve tube, spin your wheel a few times, replace the valve and inflate. When your tyre is punctured, latex is driven to the hole and, solidifying almost instantly, will block it very effectively: often the first you will know about the puncture is a tell-tell white stain left on the tyre by excess fluid. The fix works because of latex's peculiar physical properties: it will stay liquid at high pressure or low pressure, but on moving from one to another (for example, through a hole in your tyre) it will rapidly solidify and then remain stable. This process is called "Quick Break".

⊛ ETHICAL BIKE BUYING ⊛

Don't buy a stolen bike! The website *bikesoup.co.uk* offers a sensible checklist of things to watch for when you're buying a second-hand machine.

1. Does the seller know much about the bike?
2. Can they answer your questions about its history and the way it's been ridden?
3. Is the price too good to be true?
4. Are communications clear and does the vendor have a verifiable address, employer or landline number?
5. Does the bike come with supporting paperwork?
6. Does the vendor claim to be selling it on behalf of "a friend"?
7. Will they send you a photo of the frame number so that you can check if it's been recorded as stolen?

Finally, if you conclude that the seller is respectable, formalize the sale with an invoice (you can download a useful form at *bikesoup.co.uk/pdf/ bikesoup-invoice.pdf*). An honest vendor won't have any objection to this.

⊛ TOUGH TRIANGLES ⊛

The rear triangle of a conventional bike – comprising the seatstays, chain stays, seat tube and rear axle – makes a tetrahedron, the simplest and strongest of all three-dimensional structures, and the same pattern that diamond crystals form.

⊛ SOMETHING'S GOT TO CHANGE ⊛

The Croce D'Aune is an unremarkable low pass on a side road about 100Km north of Venice, but we all owe it a debt of thanks, for it was a frustrating moment here that changed the course of cycling technology forever. One Tullio Campagnolo, leading a race up the pass in November 1927, had to dismount to remove his rear wheel and change gears (racing bikes of the time having flip-flop hubs: a low gear on one side of the rear wheel, a high gear on the other). His cold fingers fumbled with the wingnuts, and he lost valuable time. On his return he devised the quick release bolt, on the same pattern that we still use today; this was merely the first of many innovations, including the front and rear derailleurs that made the Campagnolo name famous. More famous than coming 24th in the 1927 Giro di Lombardia, anyway.

◉ WOODEN-WHEELED WONDERS ◉

Wooden bicycles are today mostly seen as impractical novelties or design exercises. Wooden wheel rims were, though, in use well into the 20th century: when Antonin Magne won the 1934 Tour de France on Mavic aluminium rims, the technology was still illegal, and they were painted to resemble wood.

◉ THE CLINCH MOB ◉

The first patents for the clincher tyres were filed in 1890 (one pattern, featuring wire beads in the rubber, by Charles Welch: the other, with beads in the fabric, by William Bartlett), but they could not cope with inflation to high air pressures and, being therefore soft, were not competitive enough for racers. That situation didn't change until the late 1970s, when Michelin and Mavic came up with a tyre and rim combination that could cope with high pressure, and giving amateur riders a serious alternative to the tubular tyre.

Steel spokes stretch by about 1mm each as they are tensioned.

It takes approximately 200 times more force to stretch a steel spoke to breaking point than compress it till it buckles.

Take care not to over-tighten your wheels' quick release levers: you will increase the friction (axial load) in your wheel-bearings, slowing you down and increasing wear.

If your gear block (or freewheel) is of the old-fashioned screw-on variety, rather than a freehub model, you should take care when removing it. Heavy use will screw it firmly onto its threaded boss, and the force needed to remove it needs to be symmetrically applied or you risk straining the spokes and throwing the wheel out of true. If the gear block is stuck firm and your chain whip can't help, you need to clamp the block firmly down, hold the rim at two opposite points, and apply equal force to both as you turn the wheel anti-clockwise. In short, it's a perfect job for the LBS to take on...

Sean Kelly is believed to have been the last pro rider to use pedals with toe-clips.

◉ *DOSSARD*: THE NUMBER ON YOUR BACK ◉

A racer's number is usually called their *dossard* – a French word, as usual. Major team events give the number 1 to the previous year's winner: in each team, the designated leader is given a jersey ending in 1 (for instance, for the 2011 edition of Paris–Nice, Bradley Wiggins wore 31 and the rest of Team Sky numbers 32–38).

◉ PRETTY YOUNG LADIES ◉

The cycling boom of the 1880s and 1890s saw riders take to the stage for the first time as entertainers and trick cyclists: one of the top acts was Kaufman's Cycling Beauties: 'six, pretty, young ladies who perform some wonderful feats upon the bicycle'. Being performers, they were free of the cumbersome conventional dress of the time, and wore, instead, skin-tight body suits that look eminently practical to modern eyes and created a stir at the time. Their 'magnitude and picturesque beauty' won Kaufman's Beauties a six-month residency at the London Hippodrome, and they toured internationally to great acclaim. Another famous trickster was Hatsley, The Boy Wonder, who brought his act to a climax riding a unicycle while playing trombone - on the high wire.

◉ RADBALL ◉

Best-known in the German-speaking world, Radball (or Cycle Ball) is a version of indoor football played by bike riders. Teams of two, mounted on fixies without brakes, are allowed to control the ball (smaller than a regular football, and stuffed with horsehair) with their bikes, but not their feet: if they touch the ground, they have to retreat to their own goal-line. Riders display an impressive range of balances , track stands, and flicks of the front wheel, and shots are surprisingly fierce. The UCI supports a world championship competition, which the Pospíšil brothers of Czechoslovakia won no fewer than 20 times between 1965 and 1988, and in Germany there are more registered indoor cyclists – competing in either Radball or Artistic Cycling – than outdoor cyclists, road-racing.

❀ BUT IS IT ART? ❀

Little-known in the English-speaking world, yet recognised by the UCI, Artistic Cycling is surely the most skilful expression of our relationship with the bike yet devised. Performing on fixed-gear bikes with inverted drop handlebars, artistic cyclists put themselves through five-minute routines of mind-boggling tricks and balances: a typical move might involve a rider sitting on the head tube, balancing on the back wheel alone, pedalling backwards in a tight circle – with her partner standing on her shoulders. The dominant nation in the art is Germany, with David Schnabel an eight-time world champion.

❀ METAPHORS FOR LIFE ❀

"Consider a man riding a bicycle. Whoever he is, we can say three things about him. We know he got on the bicycle and started to move. We know that at some point he will stop and get off. Most important of all, we know that if at any point between the beginning and the end of his journey he stops moving and does not get off the bicycle he will fall off it. That is a metaphor for the journey through life of any living thing, and I think of any society of living things."

William Golding (author)

━━━━━━━━━━━━━━━━━

"Life is like riding a bicycle. To keep your balance you must keep moving."

Albert Einstein (scientist)

━━━━━━━━━━━━━━━━━

"Life is like riding a bicycle: you don't fall off unless you stop pedalling."

Claude Pepper (US Senator)

━━━━━━━━━━━━━━━━━

"...to me it is for starters, movement, music, departure, arrival, design, poetry, art, health, fun. But most of all, it is this incredible machine that involves two wheels, a pipe frame, handlebars, seat, hangar (if that's the spelling of the word), pedals, and chain. You get on this simple machine, you hold the handlebars, you press down on the pedals with your feet, and you go. That's what you do, and to a boy of eight or nine, going is the thing, going is living. It is experience, art, observation. It is even religion, even if you are an atheist or think you are..."

William Saroyan (dramatist)

⊛ AND FINALLY... ⊛

The winner of the Kuurne–Brussels–Kuurne, a one-day race staged in Belgium each spring, is given a stuffed toy donkey called Ambrose as a prize.

⊕ BIBLIOGRAPHY OF PRINCIPAL SOURCES ⊕

"I have started many stories about bicycle racing but have never written one that is as good as the races are both on the indoor tracks and on the roads" wrote Ernest Hemingway, and he's put his finger on one problem: for all its other virtues, the bike does not seem to lend itself to fiction. Few novelists have risen to the challenge; in the early 20th century Galsworthy and Wells reflected on the social mobility this new machine afforded, and Samuel Beckett was clearly fascinated by what the bicycle might represent to its rider, but Tim Krabbé's gripping *The Rider* is the only widely-read novel set on a bike, and recent fictional pickings are otherwise scant. *The Rider* has been quoted from a couple of times in this volume: if you haven't read it yet, do.

The following biographies, personal accounts and autobiographies, all highly recommended, were particularly useful in the writing of this book: Samule Abt's *In High Gear*; Todd Balfe's *Major*; Mark Cavendish's *Boy Racer*; Graeme Fife's *Inside the Peloton: Riding, Winning & Losing the Tour de France*; William Fotheringham's *Put Me Back on My Bike: in Search of Tom Simpson*; David V. Herhily's *the Lost Cyclist*; Paul Howard's *Sex, Lies, & Handlebar Tape: the life of Jacques Anquetil;* Graeme Obree's *Flying Scotsman;* Matt Rendell's *A Significant Other: Riding the Centenary Tour De France with Lance Armstrong*; Matt Seaton's *The Escape Artist* and *Two Wheels*. The principal historical sources were James McGurn's wonderful social history *On Your Bicycle* and the excellent sporting reference that is Jeremy Evans' *Cycling Facts & Feats*. Both richly deserve to be issued in updated editions. The third edition of Professor David Gordon Wilson's *Bicycling Science* is the source of the entries related to physics and biology. Bill Strickland's *Quotable Cyclist* was the source of some of the quotations and Nicole Cooke's *Cycle for Life* confirmed some facts about calories and the health benefits of riding. The entries on James Joyce and Samuel Beckett are indebted to the research of Freidhelm Rathjen, in particular his book *Irish Company*, which he was kind enough to send to me in manuscript. Another academic, Janet Menzies, has also written interestingly about the role of bicycles in the work of Samuel Beckett; her thesis may be easily found online. The long Joe Breeze quotation is from his essay "Repack History" on the Mountain Bike Hall of Fame website, and is reprinted with permission.

⊛ ACKNOWLEDGEMENTS ⊛

Matt Lowing showed more patience than this tardy author deserved. Conor Kilgallon was as supportive and full of ideas as any first-time author could hope an editor to be and thought up the book's title. It is from my parents (and especially my father, one of the few brave souls to cycle commute into London during the dark days of the 1970s and 80s) that I inherited an enthusiasm for riding, and I'll always be grateful. Finally, in the writing of this book, my wife and daughter have not only tolerated absent-mindedness, distraction and absence on my part, but offered nothing but encouragement, sound advice and support in return. I owe them a huge vote of thanks, and it is to Neen and LB that this book is dedicated, with gratitude, and love.

❂ INDEX ❂

*This report contains the collective views of an international
group of experts and does not necessarily represent the decisions
or the stated policy of the World Health Organization*

Diet, nutrition, and the
prevention of chronic diseases

Re
WH

Wo
Tec
797

WHO Library Cataloguing in Publication Data

WHO Study Group on Diet, Nutrition and Prevention of Noncommunicable Diseases
Diet, nutrition and the prevention of chronic diseases: report of a WHO study group.

(World Health Organization technical report series ; 797)

1.Diet – adverse effects 2.Nutrition 3.Chronic disease – prevention & control
I.Title II.Series

ISBN 92 4 120797 3   (NLM Classification: QU 145)
ISSN 5012-3054

© World Health Organization 1990
Reprinted 1991, 1995

PRINTED IN SWITZERLAND

90/8497 – Schüler SA – 8000
91/8835 – Schüler SA – 3000
95/10549 – Schüler SA – 1500